A Year Without
"MADE IN
CHINA"

One Family's True Life Adventure
in the Global Economy

Sara Bongiorni

WILEY

John Wiley & Sons, Inc.

Published by John Wiley & Sons, Inc., Hoboken, New Jersey.
Published simultaneously in Canada.

For general information on our other products and services or for technical support, please contact our Customer Care Department within the United States at (800) 762-2974, outside the United States at (317) 572-3993 or fax (317) 572-4002.

Designations used by companies to distinguish their products are often claimed by trademarks. In all instances where the author or publisher is aware of a claim, the product names appear in Initial Capital letters. Readers, however, should contact the appropriate companies for more complete information regarding trademarks and registration.

Wiley also publishes its books in a variety of electronic formats. Some content that appears in print may not be available in electronic books. For more information about Wiley products, visit our web site at www.wiley.com.

Library of Congress Cataloging-in-Publication Data:

Bongiorni, Sara, 1964–
    A year without "made in China" : one family's true life adventure in the
    global economy / Sara Bongiorni.
        p. cm.
    ISBN 978-0-470-11613-5 (cloth)
    ISBN 978-0-470-37920-2 (pbk)
        1. Boycotts—United States—Case studies. 2. Consumers—United
    States—Attitudes. 3. Exports—China. 4. Globalization—Economic
    aspects—United States. I. Title.
    HF1604.Z4U643 2007
    382'.60951—dc22

                                                        2006101154

Printed in the United States of America
10   9   8   7   6   5   4   3   2   1

"A funny and engaging story about one family's experiment in our global economy. The Bongiorni family does without sneakers, sunglasses, and printer cartridges, but develops a dogged creativity and much-needed sense of humor. The myriad moral complexities in the relationship between American consumers and Chinese factory are evident in each shopping trip."

—Pietra Rivoli, PhD
Professor, McDonough School of Business
Georgetown University, and
Author, *The Travels of a T-Shirt in the Global Economy*

"You will never go shopping the same way again! It's impossible to read Sara Bongiorni's book and not be captivated by the complexity and challenge of her task, and to then try it yourself for a day and fail miserably at it by lunchtime. This is the rare book that makes you think about how big global issues actually hit home, and it will have you discussing those issues with your friends."

—Chuck Jaffe
Senior columnist, MarketWatch, and
Host, *Your Money* (www.yourmoneyradio.net)

A Year Without

"MADE IN CHINA"

For my family,
Kevin, Wes, Sofie, and Audrey

CONTENTS

FOREWORD

China. A country with a population of more than 1.3 billion people. The most populous country in the world. And now its economy is no longer isolated from the rest of the world. Indeed, it is China, not Mexico, not Korea, not India, that most Americans think of when asked, Where do the goods we buy come from?

As the Chinese economy has grown it has come into direct competition with U.S. manufacturing firms. With low wages and government assistance, the Chinese manufacturing juggernaut has captured markets for goods previously made not just in the United States but in other countries as well.

The surging Chinese economy has created uncertainty, fear, and even anger about unfair competition. It has also become a major political issue as middle-class manufacturing jobs are being transferred overseas.

The image of China as the beast of the Far East is well entrenched. But that doesn't necessarily mean the reality matches the popular perception. So, is China really the economic steamroller we think it is? Even more important, could we really live without Chinese goods? That is the question asked by Sara Bongiorni in her book, *A Year Without "Made in China."*

So, what is the truth about China? The economic data are not as clear as the press would have us believe. Beginning in the early 1980s and accelerating in the 1990s the Chinese government stopped centrally controlling its economy. China began opening up its markets, and the flood of foreign investment into the country led to an enormous growth surge in the economy. By the end of 2006, China had one of the five largest economies in the world, and by one measure, called purchasing power parity, it was second only to the United States.

In the United States, we think that everything China makes is immediately sent here. Actually, that is not the case. China shipped about $290 billion in all types of goods to the United States in 2006. More than 11 percent of China's output winds up in the United States. Only about one-quarter of all Chinese exports get sold in America. Still, that is a very large proportion, making the U.S. consumer critical to the well-being of the Chinese economy.

Chinese goods may not make up everything we buy, but they sure are a major portion. We import more than $2.2 trillion in goods from all over the world. About 15 percent comes from China and that is not a small amount. Compared to the size of the U.S. economy, though, it is. The U.S. gross domestic product (GDP) in 2006 was more than $13.2 trillion and consumer spending exceeded $9.2 trillion.

It seems, then, that we should be able to live very easily without having to buy Chinese products. But that just may not be the case, especially for lower- or middle-income families. While the data appear to say that China is important but not critical, that is in relation to all the goods and services we get from the rest of the world. For the average American looking for clothes and less expensive manufactured goods, it is a different story. Many of the goods we do sell in this country are indeed "Made in China."

And that gets us to the story. Is it at all possible to go for an entire year without buying something Chinese? Most likely yes, but you really have to look hard and even then you will probably fail. Many goods have components that are made in China but assembled elsewhere. Most manufacturers couldn't care less where the component was initially produced. They only care that it is cheap and fits their needs. Competition is king and those with the lowest costs rule.

Essentially, *A Year Without "Made in China"* is about the reality of globalization. Actually, it is not really even about China but is a tale of how the world has changed and, more important, where the world economy is headed. Almost everyone's standard of living is improved by being able to purchase less expensive products no matter where they are made. Our incomes go a lot further. Businesses can use the extra resources freed up by using the least expensive product to produce more at a lower cost as well.

For workers in those industries and firms that can no longer compete, though, their jobs have been lost. Would they be willing to buy fewer goods because the prices are higher in order to preserve their jobs? The answer is yes. But for the rest of us, we don't want to pay more and we vote with our dollars. We buy cheaper products regardless of where they are produced. And for now at least, many of those goods come from China.

So living without foreign products may be an option, but it is not a very realistic one. In the 1950s, it was *Made in Japan* that worried our manufacturing firms. Now it is *Made in China*. In the future, it could be *Made Somewhere Else*.

—JOEL L. NAROFF
President, Naroff Economic Advisors, Inc.
Chief Economist, Commerce Bank

ACKNOWLEDGMENTS

Many people deserve special thanks for insights and suggestions that greatly improved the manuscript.

Debra Englander and Greg Friedman of John Wiley & Sons, Inc. guided me through the publishing process with good-humored expertise.

My agent, Theron Raines, gave generously of his time and experience in reading the chapters, fine-tuning my storytelling with a light touch, and encouraging me at every step.

My wonderful friend and fellow writer Renee Bacher Smith provided editing suggestions, publicity contacts and enthusiasm that made writing the book a joy. I could not have done it without her.

With characteristic kindness, my parents, Lois and Lars Hellberg, turned over their home to my family and me for two weeks so I would have a quiet place to write several chapters. My brothers and sisters-in-law, Mike Hellberg and Evanna Gleason and Dan Hellberg and Lauren Choi, provided help in many forms, including tracking China-related news for me and helping me prepare the final draft of the manuscript.

I would like to thank Danny Heitman, Maggie Heyn Richardson, and Michele Weldon for their suggestions on how to tell our story. Charles Richard and Barbara Clark provided essential early momentum for the book.

Friends old and new helped me in many ways. I would like to thank Cindy and Dominique Desmet, June and Mark Fabiani, Ed Smith, Hannah Smith, Chuck Jaffe, Sheelagh O'Leary, Mikel Moran, Shannon Kelly, Pamela Whiting, Caroline Kennedy Stone, Maribel Dietz, Jordan Kellman, Rick and Susan Moreland, Tara Jeanise, John

Richardson, Carolyn Pione, Wayne Parent, Pietra Rivoli, Sarah Baird, Elise and Mike Decoteau, the Perkins and Kelly families, and Mukul and Lisa Verma.

Wes and Sofie Bongiorni were patient with me on days when I spent long hours at the computer. Audrey showed extraordinary consideration for a baby, sleeping for much of her first weeks of life while I made final tweaks and wrote the introduction.

Finally, I would like to thank my husband Kevin Bongiorni, who entertained our children for days on end so I could write, helped me recall key events, and generally took good sportsmanship to a new level. He provided much of the book's most lively developments, simply by being himself.

INTRODUCTION

Last Christmas, my son made a declaration that would have stopped me cold during our family's yearlong boycott of Chinese goods.

"I'm going to ask Santa for a skateboard," he said. "It's the only thing I want."

My seven-year-old's declaration would have brought on an episode of parental angst if he had made it in December 2005. That's because skateboards, like almost everything else my children pine for—dolls, action figures, light sabers, video games—come almost only from China.

Trade with China is often measured by dizzying numbers or worrisome political frictions. Yet Americans' connections to China continue to grow. In 2005, the U.S. trade deficit with China was $201 billion. In 2007, American consumers were rocked by global scares involving defective Chinese toys, toothpaste, and tires. Possibly counterfeit heparin from China was discovered in a blood thinner that may have killed more than 60 Americans. Trade with China grew anyway, with the U.S.–China trade deficit ballooning up to $256 billion last year.

But the story in this book isn't about looming trade figures, politics, or product safety. Instead, it is about taking the abstract idea of a rising China and translating it into the small, real connections between China and one family—my own. For me, forgoing Chinese imports meant a running battle of wits with my reluctant husband. It meant placating my son's pleas for Chinese-made monster trucks with Danish-made Legos and trying to explain to him the difference between Hong Kong and King Kong. There were epic searches for cheap sunglasses, tennis shoes, and lamps. I realized firsthand the degree to which the local shopping mall serves as an emporium of Chinese goods. And there were surprises for us as we searched store shelves, from Chinese designer clothes to Chinese chocolates.

As tough as the boycott was, in some ways we were only scratching the surface. Our goal was to avoid one thing only: the label "Made in China." But many Chinese imports don't come with labels or tags. China is the world's biggest exporter of vitamins and food ingredients like vanilla flavoring, citric acid, and dried berries. China is a huge exporter of pharmaceutical ingredients, including to the United States, but no medicine bottle will tell you that. I do not doubt that I bought foods and medicines with Chinese ingredients in them during the year of our boycott. I could not have avoided them. The connections to China that I found to be so pervasive were deeper and more numerous than I could have imagined from merely peering at labels.

So when friends and strangers alike ask me if life without China is possible these days, I have a ready response—one formed by a year without birthday candles, video games, and holiday decorations.

Not a chance.

CHAPTER

ONE

Farewell, My Concubine

We kick China out of the house on a dark Monday, two days after Christmas, while the children are asleep upstairs. I don't mean the country, of course, but pieces of plastic, cotton, and metal stamped with the words *Made in China*. We keep the bits of China that we already have but we stop bringing in any more.

The eviction is no fault of China's. It has coated our lives with a cheerful veneer of cheap toys, gadgets, and shoes. Sometimes I worry about lost American jobs or nasty reports of human rights abuses, but price has trumped virtue at our house. We couldn't resist what China was selling. But on this dark afternoon, a creeping unease washes over me as I sit on the sofa and survey the gloomy wreckage of the holiday. It seems impossible to have missed it before, yet it isn't until now that I notice an irrefutable fact. China is taking over the place.

China emits a blue glow from the DVD player and glitters in the lights and glass balls on the drooping spruce in the corner of the living room. China itches at my feet with a pair of striped socks. It lies in a clumsy pile of Chinese shoes by the door, watches the world through the embroidered eyes of a redheaded doll, and entertains the dog with a Chinese chew toy. China casts a yellow circle of light from the lamp on the piano.

I slip off the sofa to begin a quick inventory, sorting our Christmas gifts into two stacks: China and non-China. The count comes to China 25, the world 14. It occurs to me that the children's television specials need to update their geography. Santa's elves don't labor in snow-covered workshops at the top of the world but in torrid sweatshops more than 7,000 miles from our Gulf Coast home. Christmas, the day so many children dream of all year, is a Chinese holiday, provided you overlook an hour for church or to watch the Pope perform Mass on television. Somewhere along the way, things have gotten out of hand.

Suddenly I want China out.

It's too late to banish China altogether. Getting rid of what we've already hauled up the front steps would leave the place as bare as the branches of the dying lemon tree in our front yard. Not only that, my husband Kevin would kill me. He's a tolerant man, but he has his limits. And yet we are not cogs in a Chinese wheel, at least not yet. We can stop bringing China through the front door. We can hold up our hands and say no, thank you, we have had enough.

■ ■ ■

Kevin looks worried.

"I don't think that's possible," he says, his eyes scanning the living room. "Not now, not with kids."

He is nursing a cup of Chinese tea at the other end of the sofa. He hasn't quite recovered from assembling our son's new Chinese train, an epic process that lasted into the wee hours of Christmas morning. He looks a little pale and the two days of stubble on his cheeks aren't helping. I have interrupted the silence to pitch my idea to him: for one year, starting on January first, we boycott Chinese products.

"No Chinese toys, no Chinese electronics, no Chinese clothes, no Chinese books, no Chinese television," I say. "Nothing Chinese for one year, to see if it can be done. It could be our New Year's resolution."

He has been watching me with a noncommittal gaze. Now he takes a sip of tea, turns his head, and redirects his eyes to the bare wall on the opposite side of the living room. I had hoped for a quick sell, but I can see that this will take some doing.

"It will be like a scavenger hunt," I suggest. "In reverse."

Kevin is typically game to jam his thumb in the eye of conventional wisdom. The closest he came to a religious figure in his childhood was W.C. Fields. He would skip school to watch Fields in afternoon movies on the local channel out of Los Angeles. At 16, he took a year's leave from high school and moved to Alaska for a job in a traveling carnival where he worked the dime toss and learned to speak carnie from the ex-cons who ran the rides. He returned to California, enrolled in community college, and spent eight years there, studying philosophy, gymnastics, and woodworking.

Kevin came by his rebel streak honestly. His father was a bitter teachers union organizer and political agitator who spent his weekends hiking nude in the Anza Borrego desert. I figure if I can tap into that rebel blood now, I can get Kevin on board for a China boycott.

"It can't be that big a deal," I tell him. "We don't have a microwave. Our television has a thirteen-inch screen. With rabbit ears on top. Our friends think we're nuts to live like we do, but I can't see that we're missing much. How hard can it be to give up China, too?"

Kevin keeps his eyes on the wall. I push on.

"We're always complaining that the States don't make anything any more," I say, with a sweep of my arm. "We've said it a million times. *You've* said it a million times. Wouldn't you like to find out for yourself if that's really true?"

I see right away that the question is a mistake. Kevin lifts his brow and purses his lips in the exaggerated expression of a sad clown. I hear a soft rasp of air as he opens his mouth to speak, still not looking at me. I jump back in, quickly.

"We might save money," I say. "Maybe we can finally stick to a budget, like we've been talking about for fifteen years. And it will be fun, sort of an adventure."

I study Kevin's profile. He has a square jaw and a nose that belongs on a movie star. But there is something wrong with his eyes. They have a glassy, faraway look and they are stuck on the scuffed green paint of the opposite wall. They can't seem to turn my way.

I point out that my part-time job as a business writer means that I can do the heavy lifting when it comes to scouring the mall for merchandise from not-China. If there is anyone left in this busy world with time to waste, I say, it's me.

"Not only that, I love reading those little labels that tell you where something is made," I say. "You can leave that to me."

Kevin may be too healthy to obsess over such details, but we both know that I am not. I have checked the labels on almost everything we own over the past couple of years. I take a perverse glee in tracking the downfall of the American empire by way of those little tags, which so infrequently bear the words *Made in USA*. It is the reason I know that we own a French frying pan, Brazilian bandages, and a Czech toilet seat. Those names were rare in our house. The one I spotted most frequently, maybe eight or nine times out of ten, was China. We would pause over the latest Chinese discovery, and then Kevin would say the words we both had on our minds: "Hell in a handbasket," he would mutter with a shake of his head.

I wish now that I had not been so eager to share my Chinese findings with him. I need to get him to look past the obvious, that a China boycott is likely to turn our lives upside down. I need Kevin to set aside common sense, and personal experience, and plunge into uncharted territory with me.

"I'm not suggesting that we buy only American goods, just not things from China. And the kids, at one and four, are too little to know what they are missing. Can you imagine the howls if they were teenagers? If there is ever going to be a good time in this family for a China boycott, the time is now. And let's be honest. If the checkbook sometimes dips into the single digits late in the month, it is due to a lack of money management skills, not a shortage of cash. Not everybody can afford a China boycott, but on your teaching salary and my writer's pay, we can."

At least I hope we can, I think.

"In any case, we can go back to our old ways next January," I say. "China will be waiting for us. China will always be there to take us back."

I check Kevin's profile. He has decided to wait me out. It is his standard strategy, with good reason; it works nearly every time. When we disagree, he clams up, stands back, and lets me trip over my own feet. I remember seeing this same hazy look in his eyes, years ago, when I brought home a stray dog one afternoon and asked if we could keep it. Kevin paused at the front gate and said nothing. The beast sealed its fate when it erupted in snarls and charged Kevin, refusing to let him on the property. Kevin never uttered a word.

I see now that it's time to pull out a big gun. I try to sound nonchalant.

"Some people said giving up Wal-Mart would be tough," I say. "I can't say we've missed a thing."

At first, boycotting Wal-Mart seemed silly to me. I couldn't see the difference between Wal-Mart and places like Kmart and Target when it came to issues like wiping out mom-and-pop stores and worker pay. True, I'd had a few unsavory personal experiences at the ancient Wal Mart near our home. I had seen a man scream at an exhausted baby and on more than one occasion watched dying cockroaches pedal spiky legs into the air as I stood in the neon glare of the checkout line waiting to pay for underwear and diapers.

Then there were the standard reasons for picking on Wal-Mart—its bullying of suppliers and the blight on the landscape left by its abandoned stores, among other things. What got me on board for a Wal-Mart boycott was when I read that it barred labor inspectors from the foreign factories that churn out the $8 polo shirts and $11 dresses that hang on its racks. Even then, I could think of two nice things to say about Wal-Mart: It lets people sleep in their recreational vehicles in its parking lots, and it saves consumers collectively billions of dollars on everything from Tide to pickles.

It occurs to me that the Wal-Mart embargo is a good trial run for a China ban, since much of what it sells comes from China. I know this, because I read the labels on a lot of boxes at Wal-Mart in our pre-Wal-Mart-boycott days. Still, there is a key difference between a ban on Wal-Mart and one on Chinese goods. Ultimately, boycotting Wal-Mart requires just one thing: keeping your hands on the steering wheel and accelerating past the entrance to its vast parking lot. China, by comparison, blankets the shelves of retailers across the land, and not just the big-box stores but also perfumed boutiques and softly lit department stores and the pages of the catalogs that shimmy their way into millions of American mailboxes each day. China will not be so easily avoided.

I keep this last bit to myself. Besides, I can see that my Wal-Mart ploy has hit a nerve. The lines around Kevin's mouth soften. His brow falls. He still has his eyes on the wall, but he is listening. A hostage negotiator would tell me I am making progress because I have him engaged. Keep him talking, the negotiator would tell me. Kevin had been slumped at the other end of the sofa but now he sits up and looks around the room. I try not to overplay my hand. I wait for him to make the next move. He turns his head and locks eyes with me.

"What about the coffeemaker?" he asks.

He is thinking about the broken machine that still sits on the kitchen counter despite brewing its last cup a month earlier. We picked it up at Target a couple of years ago. It was a memorable episode because it was the first time we noted China's grip on the market for an ordinary household item. We stood in the aisle for 20 minutes, turning over boxes and looking at labels. Every box came from China. We shrugged and picked out a sleek black machine with an eight-cup pot. It sputtered to a halt one morning in November, but we left it sitting there, hoping it would somehow come back to life.

For weeks we have been boiling water and pouring it through a plastic filter on top of our coffee mugs. I don't mind; it reminds me of camping trips to the mountains when we made coffee over the fire. But

Kevin feels otherwise, and on cold mornings, when our kitchen takes on a cave-like chill and we are desperate for something hot, I can see his point. In asking about the coffeemaker, he wants to know if China is still fair territory in the search for a replacement.

"It's December twenty-seventh," I say. "You've got four days."

Then I know I have him on board. He turns his head and looks over the chaos of the living room floor. He is making a mental list of other things he wants to add to our crowded household while he still has time. I say the place is half full but I can tell he would argue for half empty. I keep my mouth closed. This is no time to argue. In his mind he's already making his shopping list and heading for the door, not once looking back. I picture a swirl of Chinese toys, socks, and shoes trailing after him before the door clicks to a close. Good riddance, I think, but my next thought surprises me. For a brief moment, I worry what we are in for.

■ ■ ■

Later, as I pick scraps of paper and torn boxes from the floor, I realize there will be additional complications, by which I mean my mother, a Greek chorus of one.

At 71, her sense of injustice is undiminished as that of a freshman philosophy major, which is what she was in 1951. Her preferred topics for discussion are the Old Testament, the birds in her backyard, proper English grammar, and the suffering of the poor, in no particular order. Her favorite rule is the golden one, and when she hears about our plans for a China boycott, she will suspect me of breaking it. She will think I am picking on an underdog breaking into the big leagues after ages in the muck. She will see a delicious opening for an argument.

"How would you like it if someone boycotted *you*?" she will begin.

Then she will pause to wonder if, perhaps, I am my mother's daughter after all.

"Is it for human rights?" she will ask next. "Is it for the Chinese workers, suffering like slaves in those awful factories?"

My mother loves all mankind, and one of the ways she loves it is by arguing with it. In her world, there are no unworthy opponents. She has never uttered the words, *Who cares what they think?* She cares what everybody thinks, especially when they think the wrong things, in which case she views it as her duty to help them see the error of their ways. Once, during a trip to the Santa Monica Pier when I was eight or nine, I watched in terror as she argued with a huge, shirtless biker over whether the starfish he had gripped in his fist had the same number of points as the Star of David.

"The Star of David!" he exclaimed to nobody in particular, thrusting the dead creature toward the sky and careening across the planks of the pier.

My mother walked up to him.

"The Star of David has six points," she said.

"Five points!" he roared.

"Six," she said.

"Five!" he shot back.

A crowd began to gather. Silently, I wished for two things. First, that the biker would not kill my mother. Second, that the great planks of wood beneath my feet would shatter into splinters and I would careen downward into the sucking waves of the Pacific, 20 feet below, never to be seen again. The day was half lucky. The biker staggered off down the pier without violence to my mother but I remained firmly planted on the wood.

"No, it's not for Chinese workers," I will answer when my mother takes her first jab at me over the China boycott.

"Is it for the American workers, then? For the ones who have lost jobs to China?"

"No, it's not for them either."

"Is it for Tibet?"

"It's not for Tibet, either, Mother," I will say, "although it could be. Maybe it should be. Probably it should be, but it's not politics."

"Then what is it?" she will ask.

"It's an experiment," I will tell her. "To see if it can be done."

"And can it be done?"

"I have no idea, Mother. That's what we intend to find out."

She will be disappointed. The wind will slip from her sails. She won't be able to sink her teeth into this one. The word *experiment* will throw her off the scent. I come from a family of scientists and teachers—deeply religious scientists and teachers. Among the members of my clan, objecting to an experiment, to the pursuit of fact and knowledge, is as unlikely as objecting to someone taking piano lessons. It can't be done. There's no ledge on which to gain purchase and launch a protest. I will shut down my mother before she can get started.

I ball up the wrapping paper in my hand and toss it into a plastic bag I retrieve from the floor, then throw myself onto the sofa to savor my imagined victory over my mother. I feel a little guilty, because it is not nice to squish your mother, even in the abstract, or to deny her a juicy exchange about the miseries of the world, especially when she lives two time zones to the west and you only talk to her once a week. I decide to postpone telling her about the boycott as long as I can.

One of the children calls out for me from above. Naptime is over. I sigh a sigh of the sleep deprived, push myself to my feet and head for the stairs, and put away my mother, and China, for a while.

■ ■ ■

The children's school is closed for the week so we spend the next four days chasing them around the house. It's chilly outside so I let them go wild inside, turning a blind eye to Sofie jumping on the bed and Wes racing from room to room on a red scooter with a Dutch bell on the handle. Brrring, it clangs, as he loops the kitchen table and heads for the dining room. I make empty threats when he veers too close to his sister's bare toes and real ones when he rolls directly over mine. I casually observe to myself that I am fast becoming one of those parents I swore I would never be, overly indulgent and ready to wheel and deal with the children over candy and television if it will buy me five minutes peace.

Wes swerves by again.

"Watch it!" I shout.

He grins and speeds away.

When he's not on his scooter, Wes is on his new Chinese walkie-talkie. He distributes handsets to everybody, including his baby sister, so he can keep a close eye on our movements around the house.

"What are you doing, Mama?" His voice comes over the handset high and scratchy, like he's talking into a microphone under water. I pick up my handset and press a button with a wet thumb.

"The dishes," I say and release the button.

"Oh," comes his fuzzy response. Then, about five seconds later, "What are you doing now?"

"The dishes," I say.

A little later, he buzzes me again.

"What are you doing, Mama?"

"Feeding the dog."

"What are you going to do next?"

"Some more dishes."

"Over," he says.

We barely leave the house except to go shopping, an activity that seems decadent so soon after the orgy of Christmas morning toys and clothes. Our trips to the store are worrisome occasions. On the one hand, I worry that we will be locked out of the market for certain items for the next 12 months, a situation that would put the boycott in peril if Kevin, who I quickly assign the role of Weakest Link, gets fed up with the idea and tosses in the towel.

On the other hand, I worry that stockpiling supplies ahead of the launch date is a cynical attempt to circumvent the boycott by making it too easy to comply with its limits. At the same time, I figure I should delay saying no to Kevin, and anybody else in the family, during our final days of unfettered China bingeing. In any event, we don't bring home anything glamorous or, to my surprise, anything Chinese. I pick up a couple of plastic storage bins made in Oklahoma and a package of marked-down Christmas cards, also made in the USA and, I notice, cheaper than the box of Chinese cards sitting next to it on the shelf. Kevin buys two pairs of Mexican jeans.

The coffeemaker turns out to be a nonissue, and a nonpurchase.

"I thought you wanted it," Kevin says when I ask him about it one afternoon.

"Me? I don't care about a coffeemaker," I say. "You were the one who brought it up."

"That's because I thought you wanted it," he says. "I only brought it up for your sake."

"I don't want it," I say. "I'm fine with boiling."

"Well, I don't want it," he says.

"Fine," I say.

"Fine," he says.

He will tell you I am the stubborn one, but I know better.

■ ■ ■

"Do you think we'll make it?" I ask Kevin during a commercial.

"Until midnight?" he asks. "I doubt it."

It's New Year's Eve, the last day of our lives as China junkies. We made lame excuses to our friends about Sofie coming down with a cold so we could do what we really wanted to do, which is stay home to stare at the television and watch the crystal ball drop over Times Square. I am giddy tonight, practically jumping out of my skin with anticipation over tomorrow morning. I can hardly wait to get this show on the road. It's not every day you decide to do battle with the world's next superpower, and the wide shots of teeming crowds of happy strangers buoys my resolve. Bring it on, I think.

Evidently, Kevin is not as hopped-up as I am.

"I'm not talking about tonight. I mean this year, without China," I say. "Do you think we'll make it through the year?"

Kevin shrugs and turns back to the tube.

The Weakest Link, I tell myself. Just wait and see.

I shouldn't be so hard on him. I have a lousy record when it comes to sticking to New Year's resolutions. I stayed true to one just once, the year I vowed to take the stairs every morning to the fourth-floor office where I worked at the time. It wasn't much of a resolution since I was in the habit of taking the stairs instead of the elevator anyhow. There was nothing to it. It was like resolving to drink coffee or take a bath every morning. The other years, when I set my sights on training for a marathon or even making the bed every day, my resolve crumbled by mid-January, at best.

There is something else eating at me as I wait for midnight Eastern time. It takes me a few minutes to realize what it is, and when I do, it catches me off guard. It is regret. I can't describe China as a friend. A billion people, a massive military buildup, a repressive government with unclear intentions. *Inscrutable,* they would have said in the old days, and they would not be far off the mark today. But China is something else as well: a relative.

Three centuries ago, my Chinese ancestor sailed to Germany, where he disembarked with his wife and young son. The trip over did not agree with Mrs. Chang. She promptly died. Mr. Chang fared better. He took a job as a caretaker to a German family, seduced the teenage daughter, and gave her a baby but no wedding ring. I imagine a whisper campaign over race mixing and illegitimacy but family lore is mute on the issue, along with the larger fate of Mr. Chang, his son, and his mistress. The child, a girl, survived. Her descendant, my great-grandmother, landed on Ellis Island in the 1870s and headed west for Nebraska.

My mother points to Mr. Chang to explain my younger brother's treks through Asia and the languid fold of her grandmother's eyelids. Years ago, my mother sailed the Yangtze, ate in decrepit restaurants, and never once fell ill. She gorges herself on Peking duck every chance she gets. Red is her favorite color.

"It is nature, not nurture, at work," she insists.

As a child, black hairs occasionally sprouted on my pale head. I spied them in the mirror from several feet away, thick black lines against straw-colored wisps. The first time I spotted one I wondered if it had fallen out of someone else's head and somehow reattached itself to mine. I plucked it out and laid it across my palm. It was shiny and inky black, perfectly straight, and twice as thick as my other strands, which were wavy and nearly white. In an instant I knew what it was: China reclaiming me three centuries and an ocean away from the motherland. No one could have told me otherwise.

Sometimes I scanned my head for more black hairs, but they were very few and by my teenage years they vanished for good. I would stand in the orange light of the bathroom and study the mirror for more signs of Asia, a curve of the lip or the eye, but there was nothing there. The face that looked back at me was as blandly suburban as Bermuda grass. It was disappointing. I wanted more China, not less.

It's nothing personal, I remind myself now. And it's only for a year.

■ ■ ■

The first day of January begins for me like every New Year's Day of the past decade. I stay in my pajamas all morning and lie on the sofa to watch the Rose Parade on television, waiting for glimpses of the snow-capped San Bernardinos in the distance. Kevin and the children make a racket over pancakes in the kitchen. I love parades, but they make me weepy, and no parade makes me as weepy as this one. My nose stings and my eyes water at the sight of Palominos, rolling banks of flowers, and chubby Midwestern band kids getting red in the face as they plow down Colorado Boulevard.

As is my custom, I tune in to NBC so I can listen to commentary by Al Roker, whom I am half in love with. My eyes are wet and my nose is red, but Al's dry wit keeps me from falling apart altogether. Without him, there's a good chance I would descend into open weeping that might frighten the children. This morning, Al and the horses and the band kids have a special meaning for me. I tell myself that, no matter what lies ahead of us this year, there is no shortage of fine things forever out of China's reach and within mine—the Rose Parade, Pasadena, and Al Roker serving as three quick examples. My nose stings again at the thought.

The parade is winding down when the telephone rings and Kevin calls me into the kitchen. It's my best friend, an American expatriate married to a Frenchman, calling from Paris to wish us a happy new year. We talk almost every week and I am eager to share the latest news—to boast, really—about the China boycott. We exchange preliminaries, and then I tell her what we are up against with the dawn of the New Year.

Her response isn't what I was expecting. It begins with a snort.

"You'll be naked and broke," she scoffs. "You're a dreamer if you think you can fill your daily needs with things made in America. That's a thing of the past. The whole basis of the American economy is people buying a bunch of stuff, and China makes it easier for them to do it by making it cheaper. People eat up everything China makes."

I jump in to correct her.

"I didn't say we were going to buy only American products, just not Chinese ones," I say.

She doesn't seem to notice.

"Every summer, when I go home to San Diego, I load up on clothes and toys for the kids, and do you know what I pay for all of it?" she says. "Next to nothing. Almost zero. It's too cheap. There's something wrong it's so cheap. And almost everything is from China. But one of these days, China is going to get sick of selling stuff for nothing and then the States are going to get screwed because they've sent all their factories over there."

She seems to be arguing in favor of a China boycott, which is why I can't figure out why she is arguing with *me*. And she is not done yet.

"China's not doing you any favors," she says. "You just watch."

I am flat-footed when someone comes right at me, angling for a fight. Even the most benign line of questioning can mix me up. A couple of years ago, another friend suggested that we all quit our jobs, pool our money, and buy a plot of land in Vermont to start a communal farm, complete with committees to oversee vegetable cultivation, sanitation, and barn mucking. I didn't know what to say. When he brought it up a second time I panicked. I worried we might end up

living in a compound in the snow, trapped in endless meetings over
tractors and goats. I asked Kevin for advice on how to throw water on
the idea.

"You could tell him we don't want to," he suggested.

I don't know how Kevin comes up with this stuff.

I am nearly as clumsy this morning as I come to the boycott's defense.

"I think it's possible," I tell my friend. "Not easy, but possible."

She gets in a final dig.

"You'll never make it," she says.

We leave the matter there. We spend the next few minutes talking
about her children, then my children, then her weather, then mine. We
wish each other a happy new year once more, and then hang up.

The conversation is unnerving. I had expected unconditional support, which, after all, is what I have given her during our three decades
of friendship. Maybe I should not be surprised. She has been the alpha
female in our relationship ever since she moved down the street during
the fourth grade and quickly established herself as the smartest girl in
the class and the one with the best hair. My role always has been that of
malleable and amusing sidekick, but I feel there are times, like now,
when she ought to get with the program and refrain from throwing
around her many and varied opinions.

I find a silver lining in the testy exchange with my friend. It has put
me in the mood for a party at another friend's house later that day, a
gathering to watch the Rose Bowl on television. I don't care much
about the outcome of the game; I have no opinion in the matchup between Michigan and Texas. But I am eager to have access to a roomful
of friends, a group of uncritical, real *American* friends with beers in their
hands and football on their minds who haven't spent the last decade living in Paris and growing haughty, skeptical, and—well, *French*.

Things start to go my way soon after we arrive and settle in at the
football party. It is easy to harvest accolades from this group, which includes a couple of my co-workers and their spouses. This is how I
squeeze boycott endorsements from them: I wait for a commercial, then
turn to somebody and ask, casually, with feigned interest, if they have

made a New Year's resolution. It's a foolproof formula. It works whether they are gung ho on self-improvement or roll their eyes at the idea, à la Kevin. After they are done talking, I ask, "Now do you want to hear mine?" They are not in a position to say no.

Then I tell them about the boycott and sit back to receive their praise. They say things like, *What a great idea,* and *We should do something like that,* and *Good for you.* By half time, I manage to get the whole room focused on China, and our looming family battle. Everybody starts picking up objects from the floor and nearby shelves and turning them over to check the labels. Turns out, our friends' house is as Chinese as ours, but somebody turns up a surprise: a plastic Hungry Hippos game made in the USA. I am in a grand mood by the time we get home.

Over the next few days, I manage to bring up the boycott nearly everywhere I go.

"My husband is going to love this," says the neighbor across the street, a woman I barely know. "It drives him nuts that everything's from China."

"That's fantastic," says another friend, visiting from out of town. She turns to her husband, who seems more cautious about the likelihood of our success, with an offer to make things interesting. "How much do you want to bet they can do it?" she asks him.

Naturally, it's too much to expect buy-in from everyone.

"Not even Chinese food?" asks a woman I meet at a writer's workshop.

"Chinese food is fine," I explain. "So long as it doesn't come from China."

"Whence this sudden hatred of the Chinese?" deadpans my friend Danny when I run into him at a party. Then he says something else: "You should be writing this down."

I should be writing this down?

"You should be writing this down. Interesting things are going to happen."

Interesting things are going to happen?

"Something is going to happen," he repeats.

Danny keeps his own counsel and does not suffer fools gladly. He does not mess around. So when he tells you to write something down, you write it down. And when he tells you that something is going to happen, something is going to happen. My heart races as I consider his words.

Something is going to happen.

■ ■ ■

Nothing happens.

Well, not exactly nothing, but close to it. A few days after New Year's, Kevin drives to Lowe's to buy a nail driver. He comes home with one from Taiwan. He reports that there were two other choices, one from China and another made in the USA, but the American one didn't have the features he wanted.

"And I figured since Taiwan and China don't get along that has to be worth something," he says.

We get mixed results later in the week when we take a family trip to Home Depot so Kevin can buy metal hooks to hang his tools from a piece of pegboard that he has hammered into the wall of his workshop. He's never had a decent place to do his woodworking, and our new house has a room next to the garage where he can spread out his projects and organize his equipment. The children and I catch up with him in the hardware aisle, where he hands me a small bag of metal hooks.

"It doesn't say where these are made," he says.

I turn the package over in my hand. After a couple of seconds, I find what Kevin can't, tiny black letters that spells the words *Made in China*.

"Sorry," I say, and hand the package back to him.

Kevin heads back down the aisle for another look and I lead the children toward the garden section so they can sit on the riding lawn mowers and pretend to drive. He strolls over a few minutes later, empty handed.

"There's nothing but Chinese hooks," Kevin says. "But I did see a ladder from Mexico that I want to come back for another time."

The early miss on the hooks doesn't seem to dampen his spirits.

"Not a big deal," he says as we head to the car. "I can't see that having the tools lying around for another year is going to cause much trouble."

Something else happens, too, more subtle and impossible to see unless you peer inside my brain. I begin to fall in love with myself over the idea of the boycott, and not just a little. I may seem the same on the outside, cheerful and modest, as my mother has trained me to be, but on the inside I am as insufferable as a starlet. I start to believe my own publicity. The praise of the past days rings in my ears like a song I can't get out of my head. I don't want to get it out of my head. The phrase that's really stuck in there is the one offered by a starry-eyed acquaintance, who cocked her head to one side and told me, "If only there were more people like you." Yes, I think, bringing her sentence to its logical conclusion, we could save the world, or at least a few American jobs.

Given my state of mind, it's a bit of a shock when I realize, while sitting on the sofa daydreaming about myself, that the inspiration for the boycott isn't entirely mine. With a jolt, it dawns on me that the kernel for my idea belongs to a Midwestern stranger named Peggy Smedley.

I read about Mrs. Smedley on Christmas Eve in a front-page story in the *Wall Street Journal*. The headline caught my eye: "Christmas Embargo: A Mom Bans China from Under the Tree" (Jonathan Eig, December 24, 2004). The story described Mrs. Smedley's efforts to avoid Chinese goods and fill her family's holiday wish list with only American merchandise.

When I return to work after the holiday I hunt through a stack of old newspapers and sit down to reread the story. Mrs. Smedley and her husband, Dave, were tired of seeing American jobs offshored to China. "I know that when you get on a soapbox people think you're losing it," the story quotes her as saying. "But you really have to start somewhere." Mrs. Smedley trekked from mall to mall in search of a baseball, boots, and martini glasses. She opened boxes, compared labels, and burned up a lot of gasoline in the run-up to Christmas. Much of the time she struck out, including in her search for an American-made baseball. Other victories were short-lived. She found an American-made Monopoly game but returned it when she discovered the box included Chinese dice. She ended up buying a prepaid highway toll card for her husband, a gift that made me wince when I read about it. The story fascinated me, but after I read it I seemed to forget all about it, until now. I thought I had come up with the China boycott entirely on my own, but now as I read the story again I see that it was Mrs. Smedley who put me up to it.

When I get home from work, I decide to call her for advice. It's easy to track her down through information, and within minutes I have her on the line. She has a friendly voice with a distinct Midwestern twang. Mrs. Smedley doesn't mince words when I tell her what I am up to.

"You will have a challenge ahead of you," she says. "It was very tedious."

She reels off a long list of likely pitfalls. Stuffed animals, games, shoes, and all kinds of plastic things are going to give me trouble, she begins. Electronics will be off-limits much of the time, and I can forget about buying an iPod. Video games will be hopeless, she tells me.

"Every video game is made in China," she says.

I write furiously on my notepad to keep up with her.

Next Mrs. Smedley raises a string of vexing questions.

"Do you want to buy just American goods? Or will you buy products from companies that we have free and open trade with? And what about Chinese components? If something has parts made in China but is assembled somewhere else, does that count?"

She cautions me against web sites that claim to carry American products.

"Unreliable," she says. "Catalogs aren't much better because you need to inspect the product with your own eyes to see where it's made. Sometimes it's just the box that says *Made in USA* and the inside tag says *Made in China*. Not everybody is going to like you looking inside boxes. I have had run-ins with store clerks."

I am dizzy by the time I hang up with Mrs. Smedley. Chinese components? I had not considered that complication. And what countries does the United States have fair and open trade with? She mentioned

Sweden and Japan, but I can't remember the last time I saw those names on product labels inside our house. I admire Mrs. Smedley's effort to buy only American, but I worry that we won't be able to live up to that standard, not for 12 months, at any rate.

Mrs. Smedley also has a number of factors working to her advantage, starting with her focus on the holidays, rather than an entire year. And then there is her marriage to the complacent Dave, apparently content to receive a highway toll card as an expression of love from his wife. By contrast, I must corral the Weakest Link, who will have nothing to do with toll cards at Christmas and whose spirit I have been unable to break over 16 years of marriage. I try to imagine Kevin's face if I am able to summon the courage to suggest that we modify our resolution to buying only American products.

I sit at my desk and stare off into space, my mind racing. Then I make an executive decision. We won't worry about free and open markets or friendly trade relations. We won't worry about Chinese components, unless they are announced on a box or a label. I am not digging into boxes in store aisles, but if I discover something Chinese inside a box after I arrive home, I will lug it back to the mall to return it. The resolution we made on the sofa two days after Christmas will be challenge enough.

We will avoid one thing only: labels bearing the words *Made in China*.

■ ■ ■

We hit our first snag when Kevin decides to build a wooden race car for Wes. The children are home from school for Martin Luther King Jr.'s birthday and it seems like a good day for a father-son project. Kevin is skeptical about his odds of success as he heads for the door.

"I already know the plastic wheels are going to be made in China," he says. "So I am going to make wooden wheels instead, with a dowel that I am going to cut into pieces."

His first stop will be the craft store near our home, a hulking warehouse that I know from personal experience is stacked floor to ceiling with Chinese merchandise.

"Good luck," I call after him, certain he will need it.

"Remember, Daddy, nothing from China," Wes adds. He doesn't know what China is but he has picked up on the idea that it is to be avoided.

Kevin returns, a little deflated but still smiling, about 30 minutes later. He gives me a blow-by-blow description of his semisuccessful outing. As he had anticipated, all his options at the craft store were off-limits, including a Chinese dowel for sale for a dollar. He drove next to the local hardware store, where he found a Brazilian-made dowel for $5 and some nails in an open bin that the clerk assured him were made in the USA.

"He seemed too quick to tell me that, though," he says. "I think he was lying because he wanted to make a sale. I think he was full of it."

He disappears into his workshop.

When he returns, about an hour later, his smile has faded. He's made a car for Wes, there's no denying that, but praise and prizes are unlikely. Wes takes one look and announces that his father has made him "a pencil car." I think it looks more like a stick. Wes doesn't look overly enthusiastic, but after they sit together on the kitchen floor and paint the car blue it has a certain prehistoric charm. Kevin attaches the wooden wheels with a screwdriver and then they crouch down to give it a spin across the floor. It rolls for a couple of feet, then veers to one side and comes to a stop. Wes doesn't say a thing. He doesn't have to. He doesn't even object when Sofie toddles over and picks it up.

"Cah," she says.

Sometimes it's hard to thrill a twenty-first-century boy, especially without a set of Chinese wheels.

The next day, one of the wheels splits into two pieces. When no one is looking, I pick up the car and stick it far back on the shelf above the kitchen junk drawer where, as far as I know, it sits to this day.

■ ■ ■

There are upsides to living without China. On a rainy afternoon at Target Kevin reluctantly returns a whoopee cushion to the dollar bin after taking a quick peek at its label. He pokes around in a couple of other bins, then turns away empty-handed. We are locked out of a huge segment of the market for what may be generously described as junk. No more pointy plastic dinosaurs, inch-tall construction workers, or neon-colored pool toys. We will have to make do with our current supply of those items.

Still, there are hazards to a ban on Chinese goods, including social ones.

My sister-in-law calls in a panic one evening after she realizes the cheerfully wrapped box she left on our doorstep after Wes had minor surgery contains two Chinese-made Mattel motorcycles.

"I don't know what I was thinking," she says. "I am so sorry. I didn't look where they came from. I completely forgot. Do you want me to return them for something else?"

Our neighbor stops by later with a box of get-well candy.

"It's from New Jersey," she says as she hands me the package. "I checked the label."

I am horrified. I had flattered myself in thinking that I'd kept my self-congratulations to myself. Here is evidence to the contrary. I was so busy thinking about what we have been doing, which is not buying Chinese things, that I lost sight of what everybody around me has been up to, which is buying Chinese things. In laying out ground rules for the year, I had forgotten all about gifts, a crucial pipeline of Chinese products pouring into our house.

For once, I am fast on my feet.

"You don't have to pay attention to labels," I tell my sister-in-law. "Expecting you to avoid buying from China just because we're doing it would be like me going vegetarian and expecting everybody else to do the same. It's our project, not yours. We're not going to tell anybody else what to do."

"But don't you want to keep Chinese things out of the house?" she asks. "Let me take the motorcycles back. I'll find something else."

Me and my big mouth.

"You don't need to do anything differently," I say.

"Are you sure?" she asks me, about five times. "I can take them back, you know. It's no trouble. I don't know what I was thinking."

I repeat my assurances, but she's still apologizing when we hang up the phone.

I tell our neighbor the same thing, but she's not buying it either.

"We don't want to be known as the ones who spoiled your experiment," she tells me.

I am not done offending people. A couple of days later, while waiting at the counter to pay for lunch at a small cafe, the owner gestures toward a new display of Mardi Gras–themed jewelry. I finger the rows of earrings and bracelets. I slip a pair of earrings off the rack to take a closer look. I turn them over in my hand and peer at the label on the plastic backing.

"Aren't they just adorable?" the owner asks me.

I nod, and then I do something unwise, something I know better than to do. I open my mouth.

"It's too bad I can't buy them," I say with an air of regret as I return the earrings to the rack. "You see, this year I'm not buying anything from China. It's my New Year's resolution. Maybe next year I'll buy some."

She narrows her eyes at me.

"Well, then how are all those three-year olds in China going to survive if people like you won't help them out?"

I can't tell if she's joking. I decide I don't want to find out. I give her a Mona Lisa smile to indicate I get her gist, although I do not, then sheepishly pay for my lunch and slink to a table. It hadn't occurred to me that shopkeepers who deal in Chinese wares (and I assume that's just about all of them) are unlikely to appreciate my project, with its tone of implied superiority. I can't stand a tone of implied superiority. I thought my encounter with Mrs. Smedley had cured me of my self-infatuation, but I see now that embers of insufferability glow within me.

My mother whispers in my ear as I hunch alone over my plate.

You know what goes before a fall, my phantom mother says.

Don't remind me, Mother. Pride. It's tripped me up a million times.

So what are you going to do about it? she wants to know.

I am going to learn to keep my mouth closed. I am going to avoid Chinese merchandise and I am going to keep the fact that I am avoiding Chinese merchandise to myself. I am going to go quietly about my business like any decent citizen and I am not going to rub anybody's nose in anything. I am going to take my top lip, press it to my bottom lip, and keep it there until next January 1.

■ ■ ■

The jewelry store that we visit at dusk on a rainy Friday sits in a strip mall off a busy highway on the outskirts of town. A husband-and-wife team of Vietnamese immigrants runs the store. They sell elaborate jewelry, much of it made on-site, knockoff Gucci purses, and miniature motorcycles that I believe are illegal to drive on the streets. It's not so much a jewelry store as a gold, handbag, and motorbike outlet. It's my first trip to the place. I like it immediately.

We are not in the market for jewelry, purses, or unconventional forms of transportation. We are here on an unglamorous mission to replace the batteries in three watches. I say hello to the shopkeeper, then hand him the watches and ask if he can replace the batteries. He disappears into the back room.

"You need a new strap?" he asks when he returns a few minutes later. He holds up my watch, whose leather band has split in two. He gestures toward the display case at the front of the store and I wander over to take a look. He opens the case so I can see better. I have just picked out a replacement strap when Kevin sidles up and clears his throat.

"Did you look where they are made?" he asks.

The shopkeeper and I look at him blankly. Then I grimace and turn over the box that holds the strap. I shrink as I read the words, *Made in China.* Then I look at the shopkeeper, who is smiling at me with kind, worried eyes. I freeze up. A couple of seconds tick by. Then I blurt out a confession and tell the shopkeeper about the boycott. We are late into the sales transaction, and I can't think what else to do. He starts to laugh.

"Yes, you are right, everything is from China," he says. He tells us he's noticed that Vietnam also is saturated with Chinese goods.

"When I go home it's everywhere you look," he adds. "China, China, China."

We pay for the batteries and head out into the rain. As we make our way across the wet parking lot, Kevin apologizes for butting in.

"I just thought you'd better check the strap," he says.

"Are you kidding? I'm glad you reminded me," I say. "It would have been worse to have to drive back later and explain why I was returning it."

We settle into the car and Kevin backs out of our space. Then I think of something else. "Did you happen to ask where the watch batteries are from?" I ask.

Kevin shakes his head.

"I thought about that, but I didn't want to sound like a jerk," he says.

No matter, I think. I will call the store later, after I come up with a way to ask about the origins of the batteries that doesn't sound ridiculous. It may take some doing, but I'll come up with something. And maybe we'll get lucky. Maybe they will be from Poland or Mexico, or even America. Batteries seem American, I tell myself, in a way that video games seem Chinese. No worries. I'll sort it out later.

As Kevin accelerates into traffic, I take a look at his profile. Handsome as a movie star and devoted to the China boycott. What more could you ask for? It was cruel of me to dub him the Weakest Link, even if I kept it to myself.

I sit back in my seat and turn to gaze at the streets silver with rain. I don't know what I was so worried about. A China boycott had seemed like such a big deal before we got started, but there's nothing to it, really. You check the labels, you say no, thank you. Everybody smiles and nods. One month down. Eleven to go.

Piece of cake.

CHAPTER

TWO

Red Shoes

I begin the day with a foolish question.

"What in the world is going on here?" I ask.

It's seven o'clock on a Monday morning and I am hunched down in front of the sofa trying to jam my son Wes's foot into his sneaker while he watches *Clifford the Big Red Dog* with the slack-jawed look of a zombie. We are running late due to a predictable string of events, including my having to chase the baby through several rooms before cornering her and stuffing her into tights and a dress. I don't bother with her shoes, since I know she will yank them off in the car on the ride to school. Getting Wes's feet into sneakers is my last hurdle before making a dash for the door.

My question is foolish because I know perfectly well what is going on. There's no mystery at work here. Wes's feet have grown too big for his shoes.

I finish stuffing his foot into his shoe and try to locate the end of his toes with my thumb. He had about half an inch to go when I checked the last time, which seems like only a couple of weeks ago. Even yesterday I had no problem getting his shoes on. Yet this morning there can't be more than an eighth of an inch left between his big toe and the end of his shoe, even when he's sitting down. I figure by lunchtime, after a snack and three more hours of growing, his toes will be pressing against the reinforced ends of his sneakers. Then the process of foot deformation will begin.

A knot of apprehension forms low in my gut. I hadn't seen this coming, not so soon anyway. I thought my day of reckoning with China's grip on the feet of America's children was still months away. I sigh and force Wes's other foot into the remaining shoe. I haven't got any choice. His entire footwear wardrobe is limited to this one pair of scuffed white Chinese tennis shoes.

I ask another foolish question while I tie his laces.

"When did this happen?"

Wes is lost in the blue glow of the television and doesn't respond. Kevin strolls in from the kitchen with a cup of coffee and lowers himself onto the sofa between the children.

"Wes's shoes are too small for him," I say. There's an edge in my voice.

Kevin gives me a little nod and states the obvious.

"New shoes," he says, and turns to the television.

I had hoped for a touch of panic on Kevin's part, but the fact that I don't get it is not surprising. A failure to panic is one of Kevin's finer qualities. He stands his ground against menacing dogs. Once three thugs surrounded him at a deserted shopping mall and tried to steal his watch. He talked them out of it by telling them it wasn't worth much, a defensive posture that had the benefit of being true. Then there was the time a bighorn sheep ram materialized out of thin air and charged us while we were hiking a lonely trail in the Rockies. The ram bounded through the trees straight at us, then stopped a few feet away. Its yellow eyes sized up Kevin, who grabbed a big stick off the ground and assumed a kung-fu position, stick gripped with both hands and knees bent. The sudden appearance of a group of mountain bikers on the trail below us spooked the ram and it bolted back into the cover of the trees.

Now I don't claim to be a particularly brave person—while Kevin faced down the ram I was trying without success to shinny up a pine tree—and I will admit that courage is an admirable quality. But I also maintain there are situations where panic is a reasonable response, like right now, here in our living room, when we discover Wes's feet about to turn into stumps of flesh good only for a life spent slouched on the sofa watching television and occasionally calling out for a cup of chocolate milk. I say panic is in order because the remedy to this morning's grim development is a new pair of sneakers. And I happen to know, as the unflappable Kevin does not, that in the current age children's sneakers almost always, maybe even always, come from China.

I make a rash declaration.

"I am going to find Wes some new sneakers," I say. "Some new, non-Chinese sneakers. And I am going to find them *today*."

■ ■ ■

I have a lousy afternoon. I get off work at noon and head for the rough-edged mall where we buy a lot of the children's shoes, all of them Chinese.

I make nervous stops at a children's shoe-store chain, the shoe departments of two eerily quiet department stores, and a discount shoe warehouse where rows of $9 shoes reach nearly to the ceiling. I peer at the labels inside at least 50 pairs of Chinese boys shoes, including Shrek-themed shoes and sneakers with flashing lights in the soles that would make Wes's head spin with pleasure. There's one surprise in the mix, a pair of tennis shoes made in Indonesia, but the store has none in Wes's size. I give up for the day when I realize I am seeing variations of the same Chinese shoes everywhere I go.

I head for the car dejected and uncertain what to try next. I feel oddly out of step as my shoes click across the polished floor of the mall's cavernous main corridor. I am tense and worried, not just about Wes's feet but about larger issues involving shoes. It strikes me as dangerous to hand off the nation's shoe sector to China, although I can't put a finger on precisely why this is so. Certainly my fellow shoppers don't seem concerned. I discreetly study them as I hurry toward the exit. They look as complacent as cows in deep grass. Most are lugging plastic bags heavy with merchandise, undoubtedly much of it Chinese. They don't seem worried about China taking over the nation's shoe sector, or any other sector, or maybe even the world.

On the way home I drive by an upscale strip center where years earlier I bought a pair of shoes for Wes. The woman who ran the place made it clear from the moment she spotted us that she had her doubts about whether we were up to the task of purchasing the decadently expensive German and French shoes in her shop. I ended up spending $65 for a pair of baby shoes to prove that woman wouldn't get the best of me, which is precisely what she did get. Much later, when I thought to look at the label inside the shoes, I discovered they were made in Indonesia. They were German in name only. After that episode, I went discount when it came to covering the children's feet, and so they wore nothing but Chinese shoes.

The memory of my visit to the fancy shoe shop provides this afternoon's one bright spot. As I pass by, I take a quick glance out the car window and see that the store is dark, out of business, its cheerful sign gone forever. My mother would tell me it's not nice to celebrate others' misfortunes, and she herself never indulges in that particular pleasure, but sometimes I can't help myself. I conjure a hologram of the woman beside me in the car. *Serves you right,* I tell her.

■ ■ ■

I discover a simmering rebellion over Chinese toys a couple of nights later, after dinner. I walk into the living room and find a forlorn Wes sitting on the sofa, cross-armed and pouty. He's itching for a fight. Maybe his feet are starting to hurt. Or worse—maybe his toes have begun to curl up at the ends.

"You'll have to talk to your mother about that," I hear Kevin tell

Wes. I don't like the sound of that. I settle onto the arm of the sofa and tousle Wes's hair with my fingers.

"What's wrong?" I ask him.

He shakes his head free of my fingers and turns to glare at me.

"I want to start buying China things," he says. "I want an Alligator Dentist, but Daddy says it's from China and I can't have it."

Alligator Dentist is a game that involves pressing down the teeth of a plastic alligator, one tooth at a time, until its mouth suddenly snaps closed. The idea is to get your fingers out of the way before the teeth pinch them. It's addictive. I played a dozen rounds by myself weeks earlier at a friend's house. I checked the underside of the alligator, on the outside chance that it was from someplace other than China. It wasn't.

Out of the corner of my eye I see Kevin watching me. I feel a challenge in his gaze. He is eager to see how I am going to handle this, or maybe not handle this. I turn to look into Wes's eyes, which have grown bigger and rounder since dinner.

"This year we can buy German things, and American things, and Japanese things, and things from other places all over the world, but we cannot buy things from China," I tell him. "And since Alligator Dentist is from China, we can't get it this year. We can get Alligator Dentist next year. If you are good."

"When is next year?" he asks.

"A long time from now," I say.

"But what do we do for now?"

"We wait," I tell him. "And we play with the toys we already have. Christmas was six weeks ago. You are fully loaded in the toy department."

I gesture toward the minefield of Legos, toy cars, and pointy plastic animals that litters the living room floor. Wes turns to take in the view, then looks back at me as if he hasn't seen a thing. He doesn't like my answer but I've turned him numb.

That was easy, I think. Too easy. And in a flash of clarity I know why. It's early in the game for Wes, too. He hasn't yet fully developed his platform for a pro-China counterrebellion. I change the subject.

"Would you like to go to the zoo tomorrow?" I ask.

He smiles and nods. Kevin is still watching me. I'm on thin ice, but the toy war is averted for now.

■ ■ ■

We go to the zoo on Saturday and then to the circus on Sunday.

"Look at it, Mama," Wes says, pointing to a cluster of glow sticks, hats, and gaudy T-shirts. He's got a dreamy look in his eyes. "A sword."

It's five minutes until show time and we should find our section. I bought two tickets to the circus so Wes and I could see the spectacle of elephants, clowns, and a jeep running over a strongman named Hercules, but trinkets from China have grabbed Wes's attention even before we've made it into the arena to find our seats. Wild-eyed, oversugared children jostle us, most decked out with glowing, whirring souvenirs and fuzzy pink cones of cotton candy. A voice over the intercom beckons the crowd to enter the arena and find their places so the show can begin.

"Please can I have it, Mama?" Wes asks me. He tugs at my arm with one hand and points to the back of the souvenir stand with the other. "Did you see it? It's a sword. A real one. Please, please, please, please?"

I follow Wes's finger to a bright green sword in a plastic sheath. A handwritten note affixed to the rack says $15.

Don't get me wrong. I am sympathetic to a boy's feelings about a sword, especially one that comes in its own sheath. Especially when the boy filled with longing is wearing dangerously small shoes. But there is no way I'm shelling out $15 for a piece of flimsy green plastic, and I don't need to lift the sword off its hook and inspect it in the glare of the fluorescent lights to tell you where it was made. I wasn't born yesterday. That sword has *Made in China* written all over it. All the same, I am the one with the hang-up over things made in China, not Wes. Wes never bought into the boycott. He doesn't know what a boycott is. He doesn't even know what China is.

I need to think fast. I crouch down to negotiate with Wes at his eye level.

"I can't buy you the sword because this year I am not buying China things," I say. "But if you really want it, I will buy it and you can pay me back when we get home, with your birthday money. That way you'll be buying it, not me."

Wes frowns. He isn't sure he likes the direction I'm heading, especially when I add that his money box will be empty after our transaction.

"You have sixteen dollars in your money box, and the sword costs fifteen, plus tax, so that means you will be cleared out until your next birthday," I tell him. "At least."

I watch Wes wilt under the barrage of cold, hard financial facts. Then I think of his poor feet, crammed into his tennis shoes, and I decide that maybe it's not fair to put such a big decision on the shoulders of such a little guy. So I sweeten the deal. In fact, I make it irresistible. I tell him that I'll buy him a toy from someplace else, any toy from any place that isn't China, if he'll give up the Chinese sword.

"And then you can keep your money," I add.

He brightens. He wasn't born yesterday either. He takes another quick look at the sword, but I can see it slipping out of his grasp. He's already thinking of something else. I grab his hand and we hurry into the arena, just as the lights dim and the music begins.

■ ■ ■

A day later a child's voice calls out my name as I am strolling through our neighborhood after dinner. I look up to see our neighbors' 12-year-old daughter waving me over to the fence of her front yard.

"My dad went to Wal-Mart today," she tells me when I'm close enough to hear. She's breathy and conspiratorial, thrilled to be snitching on a grown-up. "Do you know what he did there? He bought shoes for Ike."

She pauses for dramatic effect.

"From *China*," she confides in a stage whisper.

Her father wanders out of the gloom to say hello, in time to catch the last of what she's telling me. He looks sheepish. He's apologizing before I have a chance to tell him he doesn't need to apologize, to me or anybody else.

"I don't feel good about it," he says. "But it's true."

Our neighbor has a mortgage and three kids. He's a bear of a man with a hardscrabble past, an art professor who paints beautiful pictures of birds. Like Kevin, he relishes a conversation in which all agree the nation is going straight to hell, sped along by the national addiction to Wal-Mart. He had given me a thumbs-up when he heard about our China boycott, then told me he was going to swear off Wal-Mart for good this year. Now he's spilling his guts about succumbing to the siren call of "Low Prices" because he couldn't afford the $70 running shoes he found at the local sports store down the street.

"I just couldn't do it, not for an eight-year-old kid," he tells me. "So I drove to Wal-Mart and bought some shoes there, and now I feel terrible."

He's beaten down, like he's committed some dread deed. I can't think of a thing to say, so I stand there, hoping the world will suddenly explode in a fireball and take me with it, or that I can at least think of something funny to say to break the tension.

"I just thought you should know," he says, and turns to slump back toward the house.

His daughter gazes after him, triumphant. I stand there for a few moments in the twilight, horrified to think that now I've become confessor to my neighbor. Later that night, it occurs to me that I could have made my own guilty confession. I should have shouted after him in the darkness that I maim the tender feet of firstborn children with too-small shoes, so who in the world am I to stand in judgment of Wal-Mart shoppers?

■ ■ ■

It takes two weeks but I finally find sneakers for Wes. They have a space-age look to them, with straps and Velcro instead of laces, and they were made in Italy. The price after catalog shipping charges is $68, which is about what a family in Afghanistan brings home in a month. And therein lies the problem.

I am susceptible to spells of consumer rigor mortis. A depressing television show on Africa or a story in the newspaper about starving children derails my mindless spending for weeks. Consider the effect of my National Geographic map of Afghanistan. The map is covered with dots and wiggly lines, like any map, and includes little boxes with details on the people of Afghanistan and its neighbors. The first time I looked at the map I spent the better part of an hour reading and then rereading the bits of information in those boxes. They were a succinct collection of human misery that has been stuck in my head ever since, resurfacing at the most inconvenient times.

I can tell you, for instance, that the average Afghan gets to roam the earth for 46 years, while just to the north Tajiks get to hang around for 64. Just 3 in 10 Afghans can read, compared to bookwormish Tajikistan, where 98 percent of the people are literate. But it's the numbers about poverty that really bog me down. The average Tajik brings home $1,100 a year. In Afghanistan, the typical citizen brings home just $800. I have developed an odd habit. When I come across something interesting in a catalog or a store window, I do a fast comparison of its price tag to per capita income in Afghanistan. A $60 pair of jeans? Nearly a month's salary in Afghanistan. A $150 quilt? Two months' salary. The sandwich I just ordered for lunch? I'd rather not think about that. My habit is great for my math skills but tangles me up at the mall. I find I lose my appetite for feeding the beast of crass materialism that resides within me.

Naturally, I blame my mother.

"It's because she's always carrying on about the poor," I explain to a friend over drinks one night. "It made me susceptible to the little boxes on the map. I feel so spoiled and self-indulgent that I can't bring myself to buy a quilt. And we really need a quilt. The bedroom looks awful."

My friend studies me with clinical detachment over the top of her wine glass. Her eyes tell me what she's thinking: that I'm losing my mind. That this can't be healthy.

"Are you okay?" she asks.

"It's a temporary condition," I tell her. "I'll get over it."

I always do. I drift away from those dreary numbers and go back to my days of whim and impulse. It may take me two months to buy a quilt for $100, or 12 percent of yearly income in Afghanistan, but eventually I become a normal American consumer again.

So it's not really a surprise that I'm thinking about Afghanistan again this afternoon, as I sit at my desk and gaze at the glossy photograph of the Italian sneakers that can rescue Wes's precious feet. I am not eager to prolong the agony of the past two weeks. I've visited countless web sites, sent e-mails to strangers who mostly ignored me, and called shoe stores from Montana to Pennsylvania. I found out that some famous American shoemakers aren't really American any longer, at least not if you consider where they make their shoes, which nearly all of the time is China. Some afternoons I sat at the computer so long that my bottom went numb. There was even a testy exchange when I called the headquarters of a Maine shoemaker to ask where its shoes were made.

"Why do you want to know that?" snapped a woman in the marketing department. "And why are you asking me?"

"The operator transferred me to you," I told her.

"They are made in China, but I don't know why you need to know that," she said, then abruptly hung up.

Guilty, guilty, guilty.

It isn't that I couldn't find any children's shoes made outside of China, but they were never the right sort. I found black patent-leather marching band shoes made in Missouri, but Wes is too young for a marching band. I found girls' sandals made in Texas, but Wes is not a girl. I found wooden clogs made in Sweden, but Kevin would kill me if I put those on Wes's feet. What I needed was a pair of plain old tennis shoes from someplace other than China, but I learned that I had set my sights on what seemed like an impossible prize. My endeavor included an e-mail exchange with the owner of an Iowa shoe store whose message back to me read like a eulogy to a dead industry. He told me that almost nobody had made children's sneakers in the States since the 1960s, and that they'd all gone to China since then.

"You're taking this a little far," Kevin told me, more or less daily, but the specter of Wes's twisted feet kept me going.

I could put an end to the search this afternoon, with a quick call to the customer-service number at the bottom of the catalog page. And yet I sit at my desk, picking up the phone, then putting it down again. I frown at the page and try to work up my nerve, annoyed with my mother and National Geographic for reminding me how lucky I am.

I catch something out of the corner of my eye. It's a no-nonsense lady from our neighborhood out for a midday walk. I bolt from my chair, charge out the front door and down the steps, and call her back to the front gate. She approaches me cautiously. I tell her I need her blunt assessment of the idea of my spending $68 for a pair of Italian shoes for Wes.

"Do you find that a disgusting waste of money?" I ask. "Remember, he's four years old. And a boy."

It's as if she's been waiting all day for someone to ask her this very question.

"That's nothing," she says with a dismissive wave of the hand. She tells me about a friend of hers who spends hundreds of dollars each month on skin creams so she won't get wrinkles from smoking. I am instantly drunk on this delicious information, and I forget all about shoes.

"You'd think she'd just stop *smoking*," I manage to say without slurring a word.

"Well, yes, you'd think," the lady says. "She won't give up smoking but she wants to be beautiful."

Our conversation trails off. I try to squeeze out more details about her friend, but I see that my unseemly enthusiasm for the topic is making the lady regret her indiscretion. I don't mind being cut off at this juncture. I have what I need. I wave her off and float up the front steps, buoyed by a feeling of sudden virtue.

Back inside, I pick up the phone and order the shoes. I hesitate just once during the transaction, when I decide to order shoes that are at least one size too big for Wes. I don't want to repeat the saga of the shoes anytime soon. And this way they seem less expensive, since he will wear them twice as long, and I can feel half as guilty.

■ ■ ■

The truck has seen better days. Its white paint is rusted out around the wheel wells and its windows are pockmarked with faded stickers. I read the bumper sticker on its mangled back end as I slow to pull into the spot beside it in the oily parking lot of our neighborhood drugstore. BOYCOTT FRANCE, it says.

My mother would not approve of my first thought, which is that the owner of this truck wasn't buying a lot of Burgundy and Brie even before France said *non* to our war in Iraq. I look around for the driver, who I picture as a big man with a red face and a bad stomach. Maybe he's inside buying antacids. It's just a guess, and not a charitable one, but I imagine the closest he's come to doing business with the French is ordering French fries at McDonald's. I mean freedom fries.

The bumper sticker gets me thinking. When I get home I plop down in front of the computer to do an Internet search for "boycott" and "China" to see what I get. I get an eyeful. There are sites promoting Tibetan independence and freedom for practitioners of the Falungong exercise program and several devoted to human rights concerns and "Buy American" campaigns. The sites are a mix of vitriol and circumspection. A site that offers free "Boycott China" bumper stickers seems overly reliant on the word *scum* to convey its disapproval of Chinese officials, while another warns that China has given every U.S. city a Chinese name, the suggestion being that it's only a matter of time before the central committee of the Chinese communist party relocates its headquarters from Beijing to New York. On another site, a woman describes her painstaking attempts to determine which companies use Chinese prison labor in their manufacturing so she can avoid buying their products. She writes that people misunderstand if they assume she is boycotting China; she is only boycotting *bad* China.

Next I enter "boycott" and "France." Here I find the red meat of undiluted bile. The China-boycott crowd is tame by comparison with the French bashers. The operator of a site with an obscene name is a champion of stream-of-consciousness expression, capital letters, and the exclamation mark. He embraces all three with a lack of restraint that would upset my mother. "Treason gets me PISSED!" he writes on a page depicting Uncle Sam using his middle finger to indicate his opinion of the French. I scroll through pages of his profane musings, most indicating a vigorous disapproval of Mr. Chirac and his ilk, his ilk being, apparently, the entire population of France. "To the wonderful morons of France and Chirac: BITE ME!" I find a few sites that sell "Boycott France" bumper stickers and one that lists companies that are French, or that might be French, or that at least have an office in France, and urges visitors to avoid them all, just in case.

My research confirms something I already knew about myself. I am not a soapbox sort of a person. I am not a bumper sticker sort of a person. The only bumper sticker we've got on the back of our Toyota is a decal that proclaims our expired membership in the zoo. I also am not a boycott sort of a person, at least not if bumper stickers, exclamation points, and an abuse of capital letters are required for participation. All of which begs the question: What exactly am I doing?

■ ■ ■

I have my first dream about the boycott. I am away for the weekend in some quaint mountain town. Someone is getting married and I go shopping for something to wear to the ceremony. I wander into a bright boutique full of modern summer clothes. Nobody's there but me and the salesgirl, a striking young woman with a full head of dark, curly hair and a slight accent. She is cheerful and exotic, and before long she has me trying on all kinds of things. It's clear I'm in the mood to buy. I pile up an armful of dresses, pale, gauzy things that I probably can't quite pull off at this age and that probably show too much shoulder and leg but that I can't resist despite my better judgment. By the time the girl starts to ring up my purchases there's a mound of clothes heaped on the counter.

That's when I realize that I haven't checked a single tag to see where the dresses were made. I reach for one of them and peer inside the collar. I see what I am afraid I will see, the words *Made in China*. I reach for another dress. Same thing. A jolt of fear shoots through me. It's too late to back out of the transaction. It's not fair to the girl, who's spent the last half hour waiting on me. And what would I tell her? That I can't buy the dresses because they are made in China? I can't say it. I won't say it. But I can't bust the boycott either. She's nearing the bottom of the mountain of clothes, unaware that I am poised to bolt the store and never return, if only I could get my legs to work, or to blurt out a whopper of a lie and tell her that I left my credit card in the car and I'll be right back, a claim that will ring hollow and false even if I have the nerve to try it.

At that point something wakes me up, so I'm off the hook. I lie in the dark and listen to my heart pound until I fall back to sleep.

The dream suggests my ambivalence about boycotting China, but the truth is we've had a run of good luck lately, if buying non-Chinese items can be considered good luck. I find Lithuanian socks for the baby. Wes gives American-made Valentine's Day cards to his friends at school. I buy Kevin a barbeque made in Palatine, Illinois, to celebrate the occasion; he gives me a copy of *China Inc.*, a book printed in the United States and full of startling statistics about a fast-rising China (I get bogged down on the back cover, which says China builds a city the size of Houston every month). Kevin buys desert boots made in Israel from a vegan shoe warehouse in Iowa. Wes gets an American-made Hungry Hippos game for sacrificing the Chinese sword at the circus. He loves his overly large Italian sneakers. We can't find a non-Chinese doll for Sofie, who has started feeding Cheerios to her stuffed bear, but one night Kevin brings home a German trike that can turn on a dime. I wouldn't say we're getting cocky, but we start to see that maybe China doesn't rule our world after all. So maybe I let my guard down, and maybe that's what explains an unfortunate event late in the month.

One evening, as I am bathing Sofie upstairs, Kevin calls me out onto the landing. He is standing at the foot of the stairs holding a small can and looking for the life of him like the cat that's swallowed the mouse. He's enjoying himself too much. I sense this won't end well for me.

"You should be more careful about what you buy," he calls up.

I narrow my eyes.

"What's that supposed to mean?" I ask, a little huffy.

He thrusts the can in my direction.

"Mandarin oranges," he says. "You ever wonder where they come from?"

So that's it. Less than two months into our experiment and I take a wrong turn and drive off the bridge and into the dark waters of the river below. I have been tripped up by a can of Chinese fruit for the children. *Mandarin* oranges. So obvious. I have been buying a couple of cans a week for years. Who knew world domination could announce itself in a can of syrupy fruit? And who knew I needed to stay alert in the canned goods aisle?

I curse myself, hurry back into the bathroom to fetch the soggy baby and resolve to do better. And I resolve something else: to exact my revenge on the Weakest Link, at a time of my choosing.

CHAPTER

THREE

Rise and China

March begins with Donald Rumsfeld. I meet him the same way I've met Mick Jagger and Muammar Qaddafi—in a dream.

In my dream, I am at my parents' house in my bathrobe, filling the tub with water, when someone knocks and tells me Rumsfeld has arrived for an interview. I wasn't expecting him and I'm self-conscious about my robe, but I figure this is my one shot to talk to the defense secretary. So I rush into my childhood bedroom, which is where the interview will take place. Rumsfeld files in, followed by a mysterious federal official named James Webb and a coterie of dour assistants. Everyone is wearing dark suits. Nobody asks me about my robe. After a series of stiff introductions, I start to ask a question.

Suddenly, it's really noisy because we're no longer in my old bedroom but in the vast, open area of an empty airport terminal. The terminal is open on the side that faces the tarmac and whining, fumy jets idle just yards from where we sit. I try to shout above the din, but Rumsfeld and Webb purse their lips and say nothing. They can't hear a thing. Then the jets cut their engines and a ringing silence descends over us. Now my voice is too loud as I repeat my question: Is it a good thing or a bad thing for American workers that we buy so much stuff from China?

Webb says: "This isn't an accident. It's a decision that we as Americans have made." I write that down. Then a dark-suited stranger swoops in and spirits Webb away, so it's just Rumsfeld and me. He indicates that it's time for him to go, too, and I offer to escort him to his plane. When Rumsfeld turns away I study his profile and note that he is much older than he looks on television. I also notice that he looks vaguely Middle Eastern and that he dyes his hair an unnatural black. He has morphed into Anwar Sadat, the Egyptian president murdered by terrorists years ago.

When I wake the next morning, the first thing I do is write down what Webb said. Over coffee, I tell Kevin about my dream, quoting Webb with fitting gravitas. The Weakest Link misses the point.

"Donald Rumsfeld, eh?" he smirks. "He doesn't seem your type."

I should have known.

Later, I begin an investigation into the identity of James Webb. The dream Webb summed up nicely the nation's relationship with China, and I'd like to take the credit for his astute observation, but is it really mine, or does it belong to him? I suppose I can rightly claim anything that anybody says in one of my dreams, but what if I read comments about China by a real James Webb in some news story, only to have them resurface in my Rumsfeld dream?

The real James Webb isn't hard to find. He has his own web site. He is a former secretary of the navy, a Vietnam War hero, and a best-selling author, though I haven't read any of his books. In my dream he was pale and underfed, drowning in his suit, and sagging under the weight of his briefcase. The real James Webb has a full head of hair and a vigorous look to him, like he could drop you to the floor with one chop of his meaty hand. The web site says he is a former boxer, and he looks the part.

The real James Webb has a lot to say about war in general and the Vietnam War in particular, but as far as I can see he's got no comment when it comes to Americans' addiction to Chinese imports. I conclude that his comment in my dream is mine, or that at least the dream James Webb is mine, which amounts to the same thing.

Initially, I am quite self-satisfied about the dream Webb's clear-eyed summary of the national appetite for Chinese things. How did he put it? Not an accident, but a decision that we as Americans have made. It seems like the sort of thing you would hear on a Sunday morning talk show. But the more I think about it, the more I take issue with the dream Webb's view of the world. Yes, plenty of Americans—most, as far as I can tell—can't get enough of what China's selling, but is it really a decision they are making or more of a bleary-eyed mass surrender to the temptation of cheap toys and televisions?

And what kind of answer has Webb given me anyway? When I ask him if Chinese imports are good for the country's workers he responds with a non sequitur to throw me off the trail. He sounds awfully smart at first hearing, but the more I think about him I can see that he is weak and malnourished, a loser who's been subsisting for months on the bureaucratic memos he's got jammed in his briefcase. And he doesn't speak for me, not any more anyhow. Everybody else may be eating at the Chinese trough but this year I've made another decision and I'm sticking to it, come what may.

So take that, James Webb—*dream* James Webb, that is.

■ ■ ■

After 16 years of marriage you think you know a guy. Then you learn that he has his limits. You learn that he is sneaky, also forgetful, and not above a cover-up. At least that's what I learn about Kevin on a fine Saturday with spring in the air.

It starts innocently enough. I am standing outside on our deck, poking through a plastic Home Depot bag and keeping half an eye on the children in the sandbox. Kevin's trip to Home Depot earlier in the morning yielded a bag of uninspiring stuff: an American hose, a Taiwanese nozzle, and a handful of inexpensive paintbrushes for the kids. I notice that the brushes look exactly like an old Chinese one that I'd seen in our garage the other day. I pick up one of the new brushes and see that part of its label has been torn off, the part that would say where it had been made. I reach for another, but the tag is missing on that one, and the next one, too. I lift my eyes to stare into the distant green of the yard and wonder why somebody would bother to peel the stickers off a bunch of cheap paintbrushes.

That's when Kevin strides into view with a 20-pound bag of mulch over one shoulder, his mouth set in a grim line of manly purpose. He's got a spring in his step despite the weight. He loves the ritual of spring mulching. He stabs open the bags with a shovel like he's opening an enemy with a bayonet. He'll bark orders at the kids to clear out of the way as he heaves bags and flings mulch for the rest of day, lording over the yard like a general.

I catch his eye and lift a paintbrush into the air.

"Did you happen to notice where these were made?" I call to him.

My words have an immediate effect on Kevin's knees, which buckle. Next there's a problem with his shoulders, which slump and send the bag of mulch careening to the grass with a thud. His body starts to shake and he doubles over with his hands on his knees. For a second I think he's sick, but then he lifts his face, opens his mouth, and displays at least 20 teeth.

"China," he blurts. He's laughing so hard he can't speak. I glare at him from the deck.

"I was going to confess," he tells me a few minutes later, dabbing at his eyes with a knuckle. "But I thought maybe you'd make me take them back."

He says he didn't give a thought to the origin of the brushes until he was back outside in the Home Depot parking lot with Sofie fussing in the back seat of the car. That's when he checked the stickers and discovered the brushes were Chinese. He decided there was no way he was going to haul an ill-tempered toddler back into the store to return brushes that cost 59 cents each, so he stood next to the car and scratched the stickers off, one by one, as Sofie hollered steadily louder.

"I hoped you wouldn't notice," he says.

"Of course I would notice," I say.

The laughter is working itself out. He's starting to look worried.

"What am I supposed to do now? Are you going to make me drive back to the store?"

"I'm not going to make you do anything," I say. "You'll just have to live with your conscience. Don't let it happen again."

He nods without conviction, hoists the bag of mulch back onto his shoulder, and heads for the flowerbeds. He starts to whistle.

I don't blame Kevin for bumping into China. I've run into a barrage of Chinese surprises in recent days. I found Barbie-shaped Chinese chocolates on the 90-percent-off shelf at the drugstore. I discovered that the J.Crew catalog sells Chinese wedding dresses. Every plastic Easter egg and stuffed bunny in the holiday aisle at the grocery store bore a *Made in China* label. I know because I checked them all.

Still, Kevin's light heart surrounding the Chinese paintbrushes is troubling because guilt may be my best weapon in trying to keep him in line for the rest of year. Certainly nagging won't work. If I push too hard, Kevin will push back harder. I wouldn't dare bust somebody's China boycott, but Kevin would. Technically, he just did. If I overplay my hand, there will be no end of trouble, and more illicit Chinese purchases. On the other hand, if I am too easy on him, if there are no consequences for his misbehavior, then he may be tempted to cheat on me again. I wish he were just a little afraid of me, but I am not sure how I can manage that at this point, 16 years into our marriage. I decide to start secretly checking the labels on his purchases, the way some wives check their husbands' collars for lipstick.

■ ■ ■

"Tell me you are making that up," I say. "Tell me that's just a bad joke."

"Why? I'm not embarrassed," Kevin says. "I'm resourceful."

"You look ridiculous," I say.

"I look good," he says.

On a hot afternoon in mid-March Kevin arrives home from work a changed man. What has changed is his face, onto which he has squeezed a pair of children's sunglasses. Not just children's sunglasses—*little girl* sunglasses. They are hot pink and black, with the word *Bratz* etched onto one of the lenses, a reference to a line of smirking made-in-China dolls and spin-off kids' show. Kevin's head must be killing him the way the frames press into his temples, but he is defiant when I suggest that he promptly remove the glasses and toss them into the trash. The worst part isn't the glasses. It's when he tells me where he found them: in the lost-and-found basket at the children's preschool, next to the parent sign-in sheet.

"So you *stole* them?" I ask.

"I've been watching them," he says. "They've been there for months, maybe a year. These aren't lost sunglasses. These are nobody's sunglasses."

Kevin's descent into petty crime began with the loss of his Italian sunglasses last week. He moped for days after he discovered they were missing. He'd had them for a decade and claimed they made him look like Tom Cruise in the movie *Top Gun*. He knows replacing them with anything but Chinese sunglasses is likely to cost a fortune, and we are running short on fortune lately. He's cheered up in the past few days after a friend at work began offering philosophical advice on his predicament. People don't lose sunglasses, Kevin's friend tells him. They place them in a figurative grab bag of lost shades that stretches around the globe. Kevin didn't lose his Italian sunglasses, he simply donated them to the grab bag, his friend says. Another pair, one donated by someone else, will surface soon. When they do, Kevin should feel free to help himself, his friend insists.

"One of your students will leave their sunglasses behind in your classroom," his friend assures him. "There's your next pair of sunglasses."

The end result of this suspect line of reasoning is the abomination that stands before me this afternoon in our kitchen, a 46-year-old man wearing sunglasses that would fit the head of a baby.

"Let me see them," I say.

The man behind the glasses is suspicious.

"You're not going to break them, are you?" Kevin asks.

He reluctantly hands them over and I peek inside the frames. They are Chinese, as I suspected, but Kevin knows the rules. Chinese gifts, trash, and hand-me-downs are fair game. I hand them back.

"I hope you're not going to wear them in public," I say. "At least you can do that much for me."

"Of course I'm going to wear them in public," Kevin replies. "I don't have any other sunglasses. At this point these are my sunglasses." He reminds me that he is under doctor's orders to wear sunglasses whenever he is outside because he has a growth in his eye, the result of too much time in the sun in his youth.

"I actually *need* sunglasses," he says, and slips them back on his nose.

Two days later we are back in the kitchen and the subject of conversation is once again sunglasses.

"Tell me you did not get into a fight with Caroline over those idiotic glasses," I say.

"It wasn't a fight," Kevin says. "It was a debate. And anyway, I won."

I snort.

"Of course, you won," I say. "Caroline is four years old."

Caroline is one of our son Wes's preschool classmates. She's a headstrong blond with about a million ribbons in her hair and as many opinions. Today when Kevin joined Wes in the cafeteria for lunch, the opinion Caroline shared with all present at the table is that Wes's daddy is a thief of sunglasses. Kevin had tucked the pink-and-black sunglasses into his shirt pocket while he hunched over his plate of chicken nuggets and fruit cocktail—"just in case somebody recognized them," he tells me later—but Caroline has eyes like an eagle.

"Those are Big Catherine's glasses," she announced.

"No, they're not," Kevin said.

"Yes they are," she said.

"No, they're not," he repeated.

"You shouldn't steal, Mr. Kevin," Caroline said, wagging her finger at him from across the table.

"I didn't," he lied.

"Yes, you did," she said. "You stole Big Catherine's sunglasses."

"Nah, uh," he said.

"Uh, huh," she said.

"Stop," I say now, holding up my hand and interrupting Kevin's story. "I can't take much more of this."

Kevin looks as if he can take more of this. Much more. He looks enormously pleased with himself. Then I think of something and my head starts to spin. I have to lean against the counter for support. I have just remembered Big Catherine. She *was* big. She left the preschool last year to go to kindergarten, which would explain why the pink-and-black sunglasses sat unclaimed in the lost and found for months.

So Caroline is right. Wes's daddy did steal Big Catherine's sunglasses.

■ ■ ■

There is no such place as Panoceanic China. There is also no such place as Transoceanic China. I look up those names in the CIA World Factbook, just to be sure, but they are as fictitious as Oz. Nevertheless, Kevin encounters dozens of inexpensive sunglasses at the grocery store whose labels claim they were manufactured in precisely those places.

"I figured those were just fancy names for China," he says. "They couldn't fool me."

I am proud of Kevin for resisting the sunglasses since he could argue that the purchase of an item from Panoceanic China or Transoceanic China does not technically run afoul of a China boycott. His will power is surprising because he has grown desperate for sunglasses again after the demise of the ill-gotten pink-and-black pair. It self-destructed the day after his fight with Caroline, the victim of use by an inappropriately large adult head. I held my tongue when Kevin contemptuously deposited the broken pieces on the kitchen table.

"Happy now?" he asked me.

Yes, I thought. Very.

I find a short-term solution to Kevin's eyewear dilemma in a box in the attic: a pair of glacier glasses that he bought years ago when we nurtured plans to become mountain climbers. Our mountaineering ambitions never advanced beyond the purchase of glacier glasses and sturdy hiking boots, but the glasses are a handy find now, beneath a white March sky that stings like acid in the unprotected eye. The glacier glasses have huge round lenses of opaque black and leather blinders on the sides. When Kevin wears them, he resembles an old-fashioned carriage horse. He perks up when he realizes he draws stares of dismay when he wears them while jogging around the lake in our neighborhood.

"People think I'm blind, so they find it amazing to see me running," he says. "When I know they are looking, I start to run faster."

Yet the glacier glasses are not an ideal replacement for the lost Italian glasses. They are so heavy they start to hurt Kevin's head after 20 minutes. The leather blinders block his peripheral vision, making him a hazard behind the wheel. He has to make long swings of his head from side to side to make sure he's not pulling out in front of a big rig or running over somebody when he changes lanes. He's a good sport about looking like a horse, but there's no getting around the fact that these glasses were made for navigating glaciers, not suburbia.

So I do my wifely duty. I try to rescue Kevin's eyes. I drive to the mall to scour the accessory racks, a trip that becomes another occasion for teeth-gnashing thoughts about China taking over the world, or at least the mall. I check upwards of 60 pairs of sunglasses, but they are all Chinese. Back at the house, I find there's no shortage of American and Italian sunglasses for sale over the Internet, but I cringe at the prices, which seem to start at $150. When we bought Kevin's Italian sunglasses we were young and frivolous, with nobody to worry about but ourselves. We're no smarter now, but pesky envelopes from creditors slip through the mail slot every afternoon, putting a damper on our ambitions to live like rock stars. It's not that we no longer aspire to Italian sunglasses, but what we can afford are Chinese ones. I decide that maybe Kevin's friend at work isn't so dim after all, and that maybe

Kevin should wait for another pair from the global grab bag to surface so he can help himself, free of charge.

Kevin's department secretary rescues him. One morning he walks into his office at the university and finds two pairs of sunglasses sitting on his desk.

"They're Chinese, but they're a gift," he informs me, in case I'm thinking of objecting. "She bought them for one dollar each at the Dollar Store after she got tired of listening to me complain."

I am grateful she decided to spend two dollars. One afternoon I can't find my own Italian sunglasses, which were as pricey as Kevin's. I check my purse, the car, and then my purse again, but they are gone, apparently forever. I find the extra $1 pair from Kevin's department secretary on the kitchen counter and slip them onto my face. I study my reflection in the kitchen window. The lenses are unfashionably large and the frames so loose that they fall off my face if I make the slightest movement of my head. I take them off and put them back on the counter. I decide to squint my way through spring and hope that the global grab bag of lost sunglasses brings me a nice replacement pair, and soon.

■ ■ ■

A bit of China slips back into the house one evening in late March. At least it feels like a bit of China. I'm sitting on the edge of the tub, drying Sofie's hair, when I notice a dark strand on the crown of her head. I rub at it with the towel, generating a howl of protest. Then I take another look.

Anchored in her pink scalp is a black hair surrounded by platinum strands. I rub at the black hair again, just to make sure it's really attached to her head. Then I call to Kevin to hurry in and take a look at the baby, who objects to this scrutiny of her head. Kevin ambles in, nonchalant.

"See it? See it?" I repeat as I wrestle the squirming child.

He narrows his eyes and nods. Wes appears in the door and Kevin waves him over, then lifts him to get a better look.

"It's China coming out of your sister's head," he tells Wes.

We all stare at Sofie's scalp for several seconds. Then the men of the family have had enough and file out of the bathroom. I can't recover quite so quickly. I let Sofie run off in the buff so I can sit on the edge of the tub for a minute. I have been working to push China out of the house and yet here is China, seeming to push its way back in, reminding me of its claim to a few drops of the blood that runs in my veins, and Sofie's, too. *You can ban me from plastic shopping bags, but I have a right to be here,* China seems to say. *You can't get rid of me so easily.*

I have never believed in signs, ghosts, or omens, but now I wonder whether I should rethink my stance on such matters.

The next morning I call my older brother, a biologist. I ask him whether he thinks the black hair is more genetically Chinese than the baby's other hairs. I hear him take a deep breath.

"All of her hairs have the same genetic code, no matter what color they are," he sighs. "Color has nothing to do with it."

"Then what made her launch this black hair out of the blue?"

"It could be a mutant hair, but that probably doesn't have anything to do with a Chinese ancestor," he says. "That's probably what it is. A mutant."

He states this with authority, but I'm not so sure he's right. I remind myself that he's a *marine* biologist, with a special interest in sea corals. Hair is outside his field of expertise. I'm also not sure I like the way he tosses around the word *mutant* in discussing his niece. And I'm distracted by a larger dilemma relating to Sofie's Chinese hair, since that's what I decide it is, my brother's dissenting opinion notwithstanding. I need to decide whether or not to pluck it. If I leave it where it is it may fall out during a scuffle with another toddler on the playground and no one will believe that it was ever connected to Sofie's head.

All the same, to see that black hair growing amid Sofie's pale locks is the sort of thing you'd normally expect to find only in a medical textbook or the *Guinness Book of World Records*. To remove it from its natural habitat seems a pity. I decide on another course while I make up my mind about plucking. I will gather witnesses.

"That's amazing," my neighbor says after I drag Sofie to her house and present the baby's head to her. "You should definitely pull it out."

"I've never seen anything like it," my sister-in-law announces during our next stop. "You should leave it there."

"I can't see anything," says my mother, after she arrives from California for a visit. She sits on the couch with Sofie on her lap and pushes at her hair with a finger, her eyes magnified by bifocals. "I think you're making it up."

My mother forces my hand. I decide to pluck. After a swift yank, I place the hair in a plastic bag and stuff it in a bookshelf in my office. It feels macabre and ridiculous and it is certainly not the sort of thing I'd normally do, but I tell myself that it's a once-in-a-lifetime sort of thing and a scientific oddity, not to mention ironic in light of our boycott. Mr. Chang always seemed a fuzzy bit of ancient history, but here he is, in the flesh, so to speak, launching himself from Sofie's scalp for one last hurrah. We'll never see anything like this again.

A couple of days later, I find another Chinese hair at the base of Sofie's hairline, as black and determined as the first. I decide to leave it alone. I've got my evidence. This time, Mr. Chang can have his fun.

■ ■ ■

There are benefits to China-free living. It's been weeks since I've felt the agony of stepping on a hard-edged Chinese toy in my bare feet, a sensation that I typically experience at least once a week while rushing through the living room. There is less clutter in the house, since after I gather old toys and clothes to drop in the Goodwill bin I don't fill the place back up with new Chinese merchandise. I feel empowered when I discover that I am not completely locked out of the market for Easter fun. I buy Mexican eggs filled with confetti that come in a box covered in encouraging slogans, like "Say no to drugs" and "Say yes to education." We have an Easter egg hunt with the Mexican eggs and some left-over Chinese plastic ones from the year before. Easter, the first Chinese holiday of the year, is a success.

All the same, I face a new problem relating to the boycott: I can't see at night when I'm working in my office. My old desk lamp died on me, and due to a shortage of lamps in our house I don't have a spare to move from another room to take its place. So I sit in the dark on nights when I'm scrambling to meet a deadline and rely on the glow of the computer screen to illuminate my papers. I try a series of solutions, including intense focusing of my eyes and propping a flashlight on some books so that it casts its beam on my notes, but these remedies are unsatisfactory in the extreme. I need a lamp, and lamps are from China, or so I conclude after a couple of joyless afternoons of local shopping.

Then a small miracle happens while I am idly flipping through catalogs one morning. I spy a nice looking lamp with a reasonable price tag. Its description is missing the telltale word *Imported*, which I've learned is catalog-speak for *Made in China*. I dial the customer-service number and ask for the lamp's country of origin.

"USA," the customer-service rep tells me.

I nearly drop the phone.

"I'll take it," I say.

A lamp is not normally cause for celebration, but I jump from my office chair and race out the front door a few days later when a brown UPS truck lurches to a halt in front of our house. Back inside, I rip open the box and send Styrofoam popcorn shooting across the living room floor. But the next thing I see stops me cold. Inside the top of the box is a clear plastic bag containing a thin piece of curved metal. And on the outside of the bag, writ large in black capital letters, are the words *Made in China*. I sink a little. No, I sink a lot.

I crouch down to examine the outside of the box. *Made in USA*, it proclaims. Well, not entirely, I think. With a heavy heart I crawl around on the living room floor collecting the pieces of Styrofoam so I can repack the box. On the return slip I write that I'm returning the lamp because it was not as described, since it was described as American. Then I push the box next to the front door so I can mail it back later in the week. I don't have the stomach to return it right away.

A couple of days pass. The box remains in its spot by the door. It's become a convenient place to throw unopened mail and children's jackets. I tell myself I haven't had the time to mail it off, but the truth is I'm wondering whether I should keep the thing. Maybe using Chinese parts is the only way the company that made the lamp—or most of the lamp anyway—can cut costs and stay afloat. Maybe without a few Chinese components here and there the place would go belly up all together, or ship over to China and set up business there, like everybody else is doing.

"Keep it," says Kevin, who's been listening impatiently to my soliloquy.

He can't sway my decision, but I know who can. I track down the number of the Los Angeles lamp maker and call them to explain my predicament. The man at the lamp company is suspicious at first, but then he warms up and gives me a fast lesson in lamps. He tells me there were hundreds of American lamp makers just a decade or so ago, including 40 or more in Southern California alone. Today, he can think of only four or five in the entire country, he says.

"It's almost 100 percent due to China," he says.

His company has endured because a family, not expectant stockholders, owns it and because it specializes in big lamps that don't fit well in cargo containers. He gives me a status report on the remaining U.S. lamp companies, noting that a high-end firm in Miami is "having its lunch eaten by the Chinese," who are masters of cheap knockoffs. I ask him about the Chinese part in my lamp box. A consequence of so many factory closures is that you can no longer get American-made components, he says. Light switches are no longer made in the United States at all, for instance, he says.

"At a certain point you have to go overseas for parts," he tells me.

We hang up and I sit and think about lamps. Maybe it's not an earth-shattering revelation, but it's odd to think that there is no longer such thing as an American-made lamp, at least not strictly speaking. The lamp sitting in the box by the door is probably as American as a lamp can get these days, but, not unlike my daughter Sofie, it's a mixed-heritage product, with China contributing essential parts. I get the same mournful feeling as when I realized American tennis shoes were a relic of the past. I feel something slipping away, but I'm not certain what it is.

I keep the lamp. I decide *Made in USA* on the outside of the box trumps *Made in China* on the inside. It's not an entirely satisfying decision. I wish I had a boycott rulebook to guide me, because one of the problems in making up rules on the fly is you're never sure if you're making a decision out of convenience or conviction. Either way, there's no time to dwell on the lamp. Kevin is threatening rebellion after losing the replacement pair of sunglasses from his secretary. And he's made an alarming announcement. He says he wants to buy an inflatable backyard swimming pool for the children. He didn't just say he *wanted* to buy a pool for them, but that he *will* buy a pool for them, a statement that is ominous if you happen to know, as I do, where inflatable pools come from these days.

CHAPTER

FOUR

Manufacturing Dissent

I remember the moment I knew I wanted to marry Kevin. I'd known him for a couple of months. We were sitting on the beach in Waikiki with a mutual friend, and Kevin was entertaining a toddler who had wandered across the sand from a neighboring beach blanket. Together Kevin and the little boy plucked shells from the sand and decided if they were good enough to keep, in which case they dropped them into a pile, or yucky, in which case they pitched them toward the sea.

My friend was droning on about boyfriend troubles with a juicy story of heartbreak but I found I couldn't concentrate on what she was telling me. I was distracted by Kevin's good-humored antics with the child, who squealed with delight each time Kevin declared a shell "Yucky!" and flung it with great drama into the waves. I'd already taken a good look at Kevin. He had a laugh that startled strangers in restaurants, a wicked sense of humor, and a lack of self-consciousness that allowed him to amble through life with laid-back dignity in a wardrobe of faded thrift-shop T-shirts. Not only that, he was a ringer for Steve McQueen, only better, because he had green eyes and a sweet disposition.

I wasn't looking for love when I received a last-minute invitation from Kevin and our mutual friend to join them on a budget trip to Hawaii. I was counting on a mindless week of sunburns and drinks with umbrellas in them. Now, as I sat on my towel and pretended to listen to my melancholy friend, it hit me that something serious was under way. I realized that the man who could give me a lifetime of happiness, someone I barely knew, was cavorting on the sand a few feet away from me. The thing was, Kevin didn't know that I could give him a lifetime of happiness, too. From my spot on the sand I resolved to set about convincing him of that. It took him what seemed like forever to come to his senses and ask me to marry him—two weeks. I forgave him for taking so long, we got married, and I've never looked back.

It's difficult to reconcile the memory of Kevin as good-humored-Steve-McQueen-on-the-beach with the sour man standing before me in the pool-supplies aisle at Target. No, not difficult—impossible. The Steve McQueen brow endures, but the humor and patience of that day by the sea have vanished like a curl of smoke caught by the wind. The Kevin glaring at me on this Saturday morning is a grump. He looks more likely to throw seashells *at* children than for them. Not only that, I notice he's getting awfully squinty around the eyes. He really could use a new pair of sunglasses, as he has acidly pointed out to me every morning for the past few weeks.

He makes an impatient gesture toward a large cardboard box decorated by a photograph of a well-groomed family sitting primly in an inflatable pool. I had hoped he would forget about a Chinese pool for the kids, but Kevin's memory is keen as an elephant.

"Can we get this one?" he asks.

His question is that of a child, so I give him an answer befitting a child.

"We'll talk about it later," I say.

"Why not now?" he demands to know.

It's an unfair question with an obvious answer.

"You know why," I say. "Don't make me tell you why."

He clenches his jaw and crosses his arms, showing me he's prepared to wait as long as it takes to make me tell him why. I pause for a mother and child to jostle past us before hissing my response at him.

"Because it's from *China*. As you already know."

I change the subject and take the children's hands. Sofie is oblivious to the tension in the air, but Wes has been watching us with interest. He knows who's the bad guy and who's the good one in this fight, and I'm not sure I like my part.

"Let's look at toys," I say, and drag the children away.

On the way, we pass Chinese beach balls, Chinese rafts, Chinese pool toys, Chinese sand buckets, Chinese mask-and-snorkel sets, and Chinese beach umbrellas. Summer, I realize, is another Chinese season. Kevin lingers in the pool-supplies aisle, looking wistfully at the photograph of the family crowded together in the ring of Chinese vinyl.

The toy department is never a good place to spend time during a China boycott, but we are brought here by necessity. Wes has received an invitation to a birthday party that begins in a few hours. My heart sank when I spied the envelope in his cubby at school, but I'd been expecting this sort of trouble. Birthday parties are trouble because they involve the purchase of toys, and toys are from China. I postponed the search for a toy as long as I could, dreading the almost certain defeat I knew awaited me. It's a backyard party and I've been keeping an ear to the weather reports, hoping I'll be rescued by rain.

When I say toys are from China I don't mean that some or even most toys are from China. I mean that this morning, in the boys' toy section at Target, every truck, gun, radio, motorcycle, dragon, dinosaur, and superhero action figure is Chinese. I let the kids play with the Chinese toys on the bottom rungs while I turn over boxes and read labels as fast as I can. I wear myself out after 15 minutes. Wes looks up at me, worried.

"Is it all from China?" he asks.

"All from China," I tell him, and watch him droop. I tell a little lie to fortify his courage. "No need to worry. We're just getting started. It can't all be Chinese."

We try the next aisle and catch a lucky break. We turn the corner and confront a wall of Legos. Lego trucks, cranes, ambulances, armored knights, robots, boats, and police cars. Not the dull, rectangular Legos of my childhood but Lego sets with heroic and even violent themes involving dinosaurs and dune buggies that would set any boy's heart to racing. Famously *Danish* Legos. At least I thought they were Danish. I pick up a box with a photograph of a rescue truck on the outside and squint at the fine print. That's when I learn that Legos aren't as Danish as I thought they were.

"Parts made in Switzerland, United States, and Denmark," I read aloud to Kevin, who has set aside his ill temper over the Chinese pool and wandered over to inspect boxes with us. I shrug.

"Well, at least it's not China," I say.

He pulls a face after checking the label on another box.

"You won't like this," he says. "Parts made in Denmark . . . and China."

We've already got the Swiss-American–Danish rescue truck in hand so the Danish-Chinese label is not a disaster, but it's not good news either. I jump to a hasty conclusion from the label's declaration of Chinese components: Once those Danes have had a taste of Lego production by fast-moving Chinese workers who don't demand decent pay and six weeks holiday each summer, they'll ditch their European factories, throw up some new Chinese ones, and leave me out in the cold. A surge of panic grabs me. What if Lego abruptly shifts its entire production to China in the coming months in a surprise cost-cutting move? Should I stock up on Swiss, American, and Danish Legos to guard against the possibility of future birthday party invitations appearing in Wes's cubby in the months ahead? Will I be reduced to making homemade crafts as birthday gifts for Wes's friends? Is no retail shelf safe from China's reach? And what about the Danes—will they offshore themselves into oblivion alongside us Americans?

Then I stop myself. I get a grip. My panic dissipates, as quickly as it came. It occurs to me that I always will have other options even if the

Lego Group suddenly goes Chinese. For example, I can misplace a birthday party invitation or pretend we didn't get it in the first place. Or we could give Wes's friends gift certificates, a crummy present for a five-year-old, no doubt about it, but technically still a gift, and not a Chinese one. And then there are books, another dud in the eyes of any five-year-old boy worth his salt but still printed in lots of places besides China and a convenient fallback if we need it. No reason to worry.

So as I toss the Swiss-American-Danish truck into our basket, a feeling of exuberance washes over me. I may be out of luck one of these days, but for now I have successfully wriggled out of China's grip on the world's toy industry. It's a heady moment. Woozy with panic minutes ago, suddenly I am dizzy with self-congratulations. I turn to the children with a surprise announcement.

"You may choose any toy you like as a special treat," I tell Wes. "As long as it's not from China."

I pause. Wes beams up at me.

"I suggest you consider a box of Legos," I add.

He points to a box with a rescue truck, the same as the one for his friend.

"And now something for your sister," I announce grandly, and we head for the girls' section of the toy department

My lucky streak fizzles in the girls' toy aisle. My Little Pony, Strawberry Shortcake, a stick-horse to ride around the house, dozens of baby dolls, even Crayola bath paints, which somehow seem American—it's all Chinese. Even the Danes let Sofie down. She already has the few Lego sets for babies I'd seen in the Lego aisle, and I recoil at the other sets, whose boxes come with dire warnings about choking hazards for children under three. We give up on a toy for Sofie and head for the cashier. I feel bad for her, but she's clueless that she's missing out on anything, gurgling happily, and pointing her finger at everything, as if we're on some exotic outing and she can't believe her luck in being invited along for the journey. When we get home she'll pick up where she left off, which was playing with a handful of rough and dusty sticks that Wes picked up at a construction site down the street.

I read the other day that China had gained eight million new manufacturing jobs in the past four years, while millions of Americans and Europeans lost theirs. After our trip to the toy department, it's hard to believe it's only eight million.

■ ■ ■

I am standing in the cool, perfumed air of the ladies' department, trying for the life of me to feel bad about what I've found lurking among the racks of dresses: a Chinese takeover of the world's textile industry. It should be a menacing discovery, but try as I might I can't manage to feel lousy, even though it was worry that prompted this trip to the mall in the first place. I've been worried about the story that's plastered the business pages lately: textile workers from North Carolina to Italy to Africa are losing their jobs as China steamrolls over the world's sewing factories and drives competitors into the dust. Members of Congress are grumbling. Europe is crying foul. African workers, near starving even in the good times, are in danger of losing the pittance they make sewing shirts and skivvies.

And China isn't just jumping into the business of socks, underwear, and polo shirts. I read that China is swiftly moving into the manufacturing of designer clothes. Chinese designer clothes? This I had to see, I told myself when I read about it, which explains what brought me to the ladies' department. I am not here to shop. I am here on a fact-finding mission, to gather evidence of China's takeover of yet another piece of my world, and *the* world.

I find plenty to alarm me. Four out of the first five items I inspect are made in China, including two shabby-chic twists on Chanel jackets priced at $250 each. I take a close look at the seams, looking for signs of shoddy work, but there's nothing wrong with these jackets. They look like something Gwyneth Paltrow would wear during an October stroll through Central Park. There are silky Chinese skirts, crisp Chinese trousers, and Chinese cotton blouses as light as air. That's the problem with more and more of the things China sends our way, I think as I finger the sleeve of a delicate Chinese blouse. There's nothing wrong with them.

Next I stop to admire a lavender trench coat by Ralph Lauren, who wants $178 for this bit of Chinese handiwork. I should be angry at Mr. Lauren for daring to ask so much for a jacket sewn by tired Chinese hands that probably don't see $178 a month. But there is that subtle perfume in the air and soft music trickling in from hidden speakers, and I find it hard to be upset about anything. I can never decide if shopping malls are happy places or depressing ones, but today I come down decisively on the happy side. The lavender fabric slips through my fingers, soft as silk. The hands that made this jacket are a million miles away. All of a sudden, I can't remember why the Italians are upset, or how many thousands of Americans have lost their sewing jobs since January, although I could have spun out that number in an instant even yesterday. It's hard to imagine misery when fingering pale-hued fabrics and catching glimpses of yourself in gently lit mirrors. I try to scold myself for enjoying myself so much, but I'm not up to the task.

China hasn't finished the job of dominating the world's clothing sector. I pick my way through the racks and take notes of who is making what. The *Made in USA* label pops up regularly among the hangers, along with labels from Singapore, Turkey, and Mexico. I can't decide if I should consider *Made in Hong Kong* items Chinese or not. I remember the British pulling out of the place a few years ago, but I'm not sure what happened after that. There are skirts and dresses from Taiwan, which is definitely not part of China, according to the Taiwanese, but most certainly is if you pose the question to the Chinese. There are racks of sweaters from the Northern Marianas Islands whose labels politely inform you that it is a United States territory.

Some labels are coy. The label on a skirt announces that it was "Assembled in USA," but leaves me to guess where the fabric came from. Other labels give mixed signals about their origins. The label on a sweater says it was "Knit in Mongolia" and "Finished in China." So where was the sweater made? What does *made* mean anyway?

Each time I see a label from some place other than China, I wonder whether the worker who stitched the label into place in the collar or the waistband has lost his or her job to Chinese competition in the intervening weeks or months since the garment left the factory. It's a sad thought and, from what I understand from reading the papers lately, not an unreasonable one.

I peek at a heavy-set woman flipping through the racks a few feet from me. She's swishing the hangers along the rack at a staccato pace and vigorously snapping gum as she inspects the merchandise. She looks like a no-nonsense sort, and I think I know what she would tell me if I were bold enough to tap her on the shoulder, beg her pardon, and ask her what she thinks of all these Chinese clothes, and whether it bodes well or poorly for our collective American future.

"Aren't you worried about where it's all headed?" I'd like to ask her. "Where do you think the Chinese will turn next—car production? Jet manufacturing? What will they leave for the rest of us? Do you ever worry that you'll wake up one morning with a closet full of discount designer clothes and a hundred pairs of Chinese heels but no job, no future, no prospects?"

First she'd ease up on the gum. Then she'd look me up and down with the same cold-eyed discernment she's now using on a rack of Donna Karan skirts, trying to decide if she should summon store security. She'd quickly realize I wasn't dangerous and handle me without calling for backup.

"You worry too much," she would say.

My inner devil's advocate might offer a quick counterpoint. Maybe she worries too little.

I leave the store without buying a thing.

■ ■ ■

Some notes on the perils of a China boycott:

The junk drawer in the kitchen has been stuck shut for months. Kevin confesses that he bought a Chinese part to repair it and then lost the part before he had a chance to fix the drawer. Immediately, he regrets his candor.

"I guess I shouldn't have told you that, since now you'll be onto me if I pick up another Chinese part to try to fix it again," he says dolefully.

We're still boiling water for coffee in the mornings. The broken Chinese coffeemaker sits on the counter, its pot gathering dust.

I feel guilty every time a Chinese graduate student at our children's school, the father of a little boy in Sofie's class, holds the door for me when I drop off the kids in the morning. We exchange polite smiles, and I resist the urge to blurt out that I am boycotting Chinese goods for a year but that it's nothing personal.

After the toy bust at Target, I buy American tulle and Mexican ribbon and sew a bright blue tutu for Sofie. I'm no master seamstress, but the whole thing takes 10 minutes from start to finish and I must say it turns out fabulous. When I hold up the tutu for Sofie's inspection, she darts from the room. I give chase and tie it around her.

"Take that off her," Kevin sternly instructs me when he follows the sound of the baby's shrieks into our bedroom, where Sofie writhes on the floor and yanks at the tutu. I assume she objects to wearing the tutu for the same reason that she refuses to keep a ribbon in her hair: because I, her mother, want her to. Under normal circumstances, Kevin would encourage Sofie to admire my handiwork and plead with her to wear the tutu for a few minutes out of deference to me. These are not normal circumstances. He views the tutu as a poor substitute for a real toy—a Chinese one, from Target—and concludes the baby is justified in her rebellion. I take off the tutu. A few days later, I give it to a friend's three-year-old daughter. Sofie goes back to playing with sticks.

One afternoon at the mall, I check the inventory at an accessory store, a place that feels Chinese the moment I step inside. On its shelves I find edible Chinese shot glasses, Chinese cell-phone charms shaped like Buddha, Chinese purses with black-and-white photographs of Elvis on them, Chinese eye shadow, enormous Chinese hoop earrings in fake silver and gold, Chinese toe rings, Chinese mood rings, Chinese scarves, Chinese faux leather belts, and Chinese picture frames. The store is a treasure chest of Chinese junk, most of it in poor taste, but irresistible to almost anybody not involved in a China boycott because it's all impossibly cheap. I can't find anything from any place but China, other than tiny bottles of American-made nail polish in blue, green, and purple.

I'd like to spend more time in the store examining the Chinese inventory, but I realize the salesgirl is eyeing me with suspicion. I suppose it strikes her as unnatural for someone to linger in a place like this and not buy anything. After all, when a store charges $3 for a pair of Chinese hoop earrings, you don't take time out to think about whether you need another pair of earrings. You buy them. Immediately. Any other course of action is unfathomable. I suspect the salesgirl thinks I'm a middle-aged shoplifter, waiting for an opportune time to slip something into my purse. How else to explain my failure to fill a basket with shot glasses and picture frames? Or that I pass on a $3 pair of hoop earrings?

I leave the store, trying to look nonchalant, which is how I should look, considering I haven't done anything wrong. I keep my steps slow and deliberate until I'm out the door. I feel the salesgirl's eyes every step of the way.

■ ■ ■

Wes joins Kevin in badgering me for an inflatable pool. He notes that his sister's pool, a Chinese holdover from last summer shaped like a bunny, is for babies. Kevin whispers to me that we've got to get Wes a pool.

"Over my dead body is that boy spending a summer without a pool," he informs me, sotto voce.

■ ■ ■

I would expect China to be a world leader in buttons—they are small, inexpensive, and plastic, and you could fit millions in a single cargo container—yet inexplicably I don't find a single package of Chinese buttons during a trip to the fabric store. I pay $1 for three pink buttons made in Italy, which, alongside France, dominates the button section in the discount fabric store I visit on a hot Wednesday in April. I wonder how long they'll hold on to their place at the top—at least in this place—before China knocks them down a few rungs.

One afternoon Wes removes a sticker from the bottom of a toy, plants it on the back of his hand, and runs out to the backyard to show it to me.

"I'm made in China," he announces, showing me his hand.

"Was that your idea?" I ask.

"Daddy's," he says.

Most of the time, when Wes remembers the boycott, it is with less good humor.

"Can we get another one of these?" he asks one night in the tub, holding up a green plastic boat. No surprise, it was made in China.

"Next year," answers Kevin, who is sitting on the edge of the tub. "We have to wait until after Christmas when we can buy things from China again."

"We used to buy things from China when we lived in our old house," Wes observes.

"And next year we can buy them again," Kevin replies. He shoots me a withering look. I try not to notice.

"And then let's never stop, okay?" Wes answers.

I thought I could count on my mother for sympathy, but she's a wild card in any equation, including the politics of a China boycott.

"What did you expect?" she asks after I complain that replacing Kevin's sunglasses with a new non-Chinese pair is likely to cost a bundle. "You can't expect things for free in this world, especially if your world doesn't include China anymore."

How many months of China-free living to go? Eight. But who's counting? I'll tell you who: everybody but Sofie and the dog.

■ ■ ■

I buy Chinese film. It's an honest mistake and, initially, a mysterious one. When I checked the package of film in the drugstore it said *Made in USA*. Half an hour later, standing next to our kitchen table, the fine print reads *Made in China*. I stand in a stupor for several minutes. Then I reach into my plastic shopping bag, extract a second box of film, and hold it up to the light.

Made in USA, the second box says.

I hold the two boxes next to each other. They appear identical. Same smiling girls on the side, same school-bus yellow cardboard, same proof-of-purchase seal. At the store I must have checked the label on the American box first, then grabbed a second box, thinking that it, too, was made in the States. Ten minutes later I'm back in the drugstore, digging deep into rows of dusty film. I don't know how I will explain to the clerk that I'd like to exchange one seemingly identical box for another. I'm hoping something will come to me as I stroll to the counter. Something funny. The problem is, I'm not feeling funny. I'm feeling worried, because every box of film in this joint seems to be Chinese. I finally locate a lonely American box at the very back of the shelf. It has a sell-by date that is two months past. I decide to take my chances.

I approach the counter with trepidation. I feel my face flush when the clerk, a chubby boy of 20 squeezed into a white polyester smock, asks me what's wrong with the first box of film. I can't think of a plausible explanation for switching the boxes, so I make a full confession. I keep my voice low.

"I took a vow not to buy anything made in China," I tell him. I point to one of the boxes. "This one is Chinese, so I'd like to switch it for this American one."

He's a charitable young man. He grins and gives me an up-nod.

"That's cool," he says. "Go for it."

I am not done relying on the kindness of baby-faced clerks. A few days later I buy a $1 Chinese toothbrush at the grocery store. I repeat the same drill as with the Chinese film. I realize my mistake while I'm unloading bags in the kitchen, grab my keys, and head back out the door. At the customer-service counter a blank-faced teenage girl hands me a return form. Most of the questions are routine—name, item, method of payment—but I get hung up on the last question: "Reason for returning the item?" The form leaves several lines for explanation in case you want to really get into it. I press my pen to the paper but somehow I can't make it write the words, *Because this toothbrush is made in China*. I leave that section blank and hand the form back to the girl, hoping she won't notice. I place the long ream of my grocery receipt next to the form on the counter.

This girl is all business. From my upside-down vantage point I watch her fill in the explanation section for me. "Did not want," she writes.

I am not sure if I should be alarmed or impressed by her lack of curiosity about my decision to return a $1 toothbrush. On the one hand I'm grateful I don't have to come clean about the real reason for the return. On the other, my request should strike her as odd, because it is odd. It's downright freakish. I have *teeth*, a mouth full of them. People with teeth don't return toothbrushes. I just spent $100 on groceries; could I be that desperate for a $1 refund? Shouldn't she at least shoot me a snide look or roll her eyes when she thinks I'm not looking, just to show that she wonders what this world is coming to?

Instead she cracks her gum, credits my Visa card for $1.08, and hands me a new receipt without a word.

■ ■ ■

Mrs. Smedley warned me about web sites months ago.

"Unreliable," she said. "Can't be trusted."

I am certain she was right, but Kevin's dirty looks and sun-damaged eyes have got me desperate to find him non-Chinese sunglasses. Weeks have passed since he lost his Italian shades. The global grab bag of lost sunglasses has let us down. It coughed up the ill-fated pink ones and the oversized Chinese pairs, but those failed even as stopgap measures. So I can't resist a quick Internet search for non-Chinese sunglasses. My first stop is a site that claims to list only American-made products, but after a few clicks somehow I land on a bulletin board of lunatic opinions, none illuminating on the topics of sunglasses or China.

"After reading about the United Auto Workers banning Marines from their parking lot and that they vote Democrat, I'm regretting my American car purchase," says someone named Cherry.

"My Nissan was built in Smyrna, Tennessee," writes Ice-Flyer. "I don't feel guilty at all."

"The idiots at the top of an organization do not constitute the people they claim to represent, just as the NEA does not represent my wonderful mother-in-law teacher," types Bicycle Repair.

"I try very hard not to buy Chinese stuff," writes Ice-Flyer. "I bought my Bose wave radio/CD when I found out it was made in USA."

This angers someone called Standing United.

"Are you serious? Car parts are made in Mexico now, my LaCrosse boots are now made in China. On and on it goes."

"I buy Korean cars," chimes in Logic. "Why? Because not one cent of mine is going to union mobsters and union communist thugs if I can help it."

I stop myself. It's tempting to keep reading to see how ridiculous the conversation will get, but the sound of Kevin rustling around in the kitchen—I think he's yanking on the stuck drawer handle again—reminds me of my mission. Sunglasses for the angry man in the kitchen.

My next try brings up more nonsense. I enter "sunglasses" and "made in USA" and end up on a Made in America web site that sells goat cheese, potting benches, dog leashes, portable headrests, and old record albums, all of it apparently made in the States but none of it remotely connected to eyewear. Next I stop on a Chinese tourist information page that recommends sunglasses and a light raincoat for a spring visit to the Great Wall. I try eBay, but its dealers don't offer anything better than what I've seen elsewhere: pricey Italian and American sunglasses or discount Chinese ones. Eventually, I find an American maker of sunglasses, but they are bulky and neon-colored, not the sort of thing that Tom Cruise or Kevin, who claims to look like Tom Cruise, would wear if they had any say in the matter.

I give up and wander into the kitchen, where I sit down at the table and sketch out how much I can afford to spend on Italian or American sunglasses.

That evening my lucks turns. I am rummaging through my purse, looking for my keys, when my fingers grip cold, thin metal at the bottom of the jumble within. I withdraw my lost Italian sunglasses from the depths of my purse, where I have searched for them perhaps half a dozen times. I try them on. They are slightly bent in the middle, with one lens coming loose from the plastic line that holds it to the frames. They aren't as pretty as the day I bought them, but they are more or less intact.

I get up and walk across the room to search the counter until I find the scrap of paper with my estimate of how much I can spend on new sunglasses for Kevin. I scratch out the old number and write down a new, bigger one. Since I've just recovered my own lost sunglasses I figure I can spend more on new ones for Kevin. After that I sit back down at the table and smile to myself. But I'm no longer thinking of sunglasses. I'm smiling because I've just hatched a scheme to return my husband to his formerly cheerful self with the acquisition of an inflatable Chinese pool.

CHAPTER

FIVE

A Modest Proposal

M y sister-in-law sounds bewildered.

"You want me to do what?" she asks.

I repeat my request into the phone.

"I thought maybe you could give Kevin an inflatable pool for his birthday," I say. I try to sound natural, like a light bulb went off in my head in the middle of our conversation. "You know how cranky he gets in the hot weather. Honestly, he's dropped a hint that he'd really like one. He may have mentioned it more than once."

"You're sure about that?"

"Quite sure."

"I thought you wanted me to get him some new sunglasses," she says. "Didn't we talk about that?"

"Did we? Oh, well, I was just thinking that maybe *I* could get him sunglasses and that *you* could get him a pool," I say. "Really, I couldn't ask you to buy him sunglasses. They'd probably cost you a mint. It wouldn't be right."

There's a pause at her end of the line.

"So where do pools come from?" she asks.

"Target, Wal-Mart, that sort of place," I say. "Big stores."

She hesitates again.

"That's not what I meant," she says. "I mean where are they manu-factured? What I'm asking is, do you think they are made in China?"

My heart bangs in my chest as I prepare to tell my sister-in-law a whopper.

Airily, I say, "Oh, I'm sure *some* pools are made in China, but I can't imagine that they *all* are made there. I suppose that's something you might find out. You could think of this as a bit of boycott-related re-search. I'd be very interested in hearing what you find."

"And what do I do if I find that they are all from China?" she asks.

I feign innocence and reason.

"Really, that wouldn't be my place to say," I reply. "I'd rely on your judgment in that case. You know the rule about Chinese gifts, right? The boycott doesn't apply."

She sighs into the phone. She's a first-rate sister-in-law, a great cook, witty and also kind. Kind enough not to call me on the carpet and tell me that she can see right through my ploy to circumvent the boycott. Kind enough not to point out that if I'm having trouble keeping Kevin in line, boycott-wise, that's my problem and I shouldn't ask others to do my dirty work. Kind enough not to resent the fact that I'm trying to use her as a mule to import illicit Chinese cargo into our house.

"I'll get back to you," she says.

We hang up.

I'm crossing a line here. The boycott hasn't been perfect so far, the Chinese mandarin oranges serving as a case in point. But our earlier missteps were somehow forgivable. The oranges were an honest mis-take. And when Wes dragged home a souvenir party bag of Chinese me-mentos from last month's birthday party, he was blameless by virtue of the boycott's gift exemption. It would have been impolite of him to point out to his grown-up hostess that he couldn't accept plastic figurines and a flimsy paddleball set by virtue of the fact that they were made in China.

Kevin broke the boycott's cardinal rule when he secretly purchased the Chinese paintbrushes, but we expect that sort of thing from the Weakest Link. The boycott is a New Year's resolution, and in his view New Year's resolutions smack of desperation and earnest self-improvement, poison pills in Kevin's estimation of character. Besides, Kevin didn't hatch the idea of ditching the *Made in China* label for a year. That was me. I'm the boycott's captain and commander. A higher set of rules applies to me.

I find myself facing an uncomfortable fact. I'm rightly contemptuous of smarmy politicians and first-class hypocrites like glitzy television preachers, but as I contemplate my efforts to get around the boycott I realize that I'm not so different from them. Maybe worse. They betray their principles for money, power, and sex. You know—the good stuff. By comparison, I am selling myself out for an inflatable pool that retails for less than $30.

But consider my position. I've reached a crossroads with the Weakest Link. He's been squinty for weeks while I stall over replacing his Italian sunglasses. At a certain point, he may put two and two together and start blaming me for the new creases at the corners of his eyes. And Lord help me if that mysterious thing on his retina starts growing again from exposure to too much sun; I can assure you that I will never hear the end of it, from Kevin or his eye doctor. Now Kevin is facing the prospect of a long, hot summer with no place to put the children, or his feet, for some watery relief from six months of searing Gulf Coast heat.

All of which is to say that when Kevin tells me he's not fooling around about a backyard pool, he's stating in no uncertain terms that I need to bend the boycott rules or he's bailing out and hauling the children over the side with him. I don't fool myself for a second that the kids would stick with me. I've seen Wes's eyes in the toy department, full of longing for trucks and soldiers from the forbidden land of China. Kevin's got me cornered. I see this thing playing out one of two ways. I can cave on a Chinese pool for the backyard and try to reel Kevin back on board for the remaining seven months of the boycott. Or I can dig in my heels, ignore his pleas, and risk watching the boycott unravel completely. In my mind I run the odds of Kevin sabotaging the boycott if I deny him a Chinese pool for his birthday. I put the numbers at nine-to-one things won't go my way.

My sister-in-law calls me back half an hour later.

"I'll do it," she says.

"Great," I say, and bid a silent farewell to boycott innocence.

■ ■ ■

"Oakleys," my friend tells me. "They make them in Los Angeles. They'll cost you a good bit, but they are sunglasses and they are made in California."

"Are you sure?" I ask. I have heard of Oakleys, but somehow they didn't surface during my Internet search for non-Chinese sunglasses, which makes me wonder what else I've been missing out there.

"Positive," she says. "You can find them at the mall."

My friend is smart and worldly, but the world is changing quickly and I wonder if she's got her facts straight. You have to be nimble in a global economy. You go to bed one night and when you wake up the next morning something that used to be American or German or Japanese is suddenly Chinese. I locate a customer-service number for Oakleys and call the company. Morgan, a young man fluent in Dude, answers.

I tell Morgan that I want to buy a pair of Oakleys for my husband but first I want to make sure they are still made in California.

"They aren't made in China, are they?" I ask. "I can't buy them if they are made in China."

Morgan starts to laugh.

"No way! We make 'em right here in Southern California," he says. "You've got no worries."

"That's great to hear," I tell him.

"Is there anything else I can help you with?" he asks.

I'd like to keep Morgan on the phone, just to listen to the inflections in his voice, which makes me nostalgic for the freeways and beaches of my Southern California childhood. I picture Morgan leaning back in a cubicle in some bland L.A. warehouse, high-top tennis shoes kicked up on his desk, covered in piercings and tattoos, cheerful as a puppy.

"That's it, Morgan" I say. "You've made my day."

"How *awesome!*" Morgan exclaims, like I've made his. "Later!"

Ten minutes after I hang up with Morgan I'm in the car and heading for the mall. I am on a tight schedule. Five days remain until Kevin's birthday party and I'm feeling real pressure to get new glasses on his face. He's edgier than ever, and making sure I notice.

I'm embarrassed to admit that several times in recent weeks I've walked by the mall kiosk that sells Oakleys. I never bothered to check the sunglasses it sold because the name was so silly—Sunglass Hut—that I figured it sold only inexpensive glasses from China. I don't think I was being a snob, exactly. It's more that I thought I was developing a sixth sense about whether a store's wares are mostly Chinese, and somehow Sunglass Hut seemed Chinese to me. But I was off the mark. The clerk tells me an Italian company owns the chain. I lean on the glass and look over Italian and American glasses that run $100 to $200, sometimes more.

It takes five minutes to pick out the pair I want. They cost me $150—more than a month's pay in Chad, according to the CIA World Factbook—but this time I'm too relieved to feel guilty.

■ ■ ■

I hit another roadblock in the days before Kevin's birthday: birthday candles.

I think it's a fluke when I come across nothing but Chinese candles in the baked goods aisle at the grocery store. I start to worry when I check two more stores, then three, then four, and come up empty-handed each time. I am not picky. I am open to Barbie birthday candles, trick birthday candles that can't be extinguished, glitter candles, bulky number candles, but every box comes from China. At home, I search the kitchen drawers and come up with three dusty leftovers from an old box, also Chinese. I didn't realize I was being reckless when I promised Wes we would bake a cake for his daddy and cover it with candles, one for each year. Forty-seven candles. That's a lot of candles. As it stands now, I'm 44 candles short. The days tick by. Finally, I call my sister-in-law and ask for another favor.

"Could you bring some old birthday candles to the party?" I ask. "I'm finding nothing but Chinese ones at the store."

My sister-in-law has her limits. She will only play the part of patsy for so long without calling it to my attention. It's not that she won't play along but she wants me to know that I'm not fooling her.

"But won't my old candles be Chinese, too?" she asks.

"I suppose," I tell her. "But that's okay, if they are a gift. Chinese gifts are permissible, remember?"

"But this is a request, not a gift," she points out. She's not being difficult, just logical, which in this case comes to the same thing. "Do you have a rule about requests?"

This time I'm the one who sighs.

"Could you just bring them?" I ask. "I'm in a jam."

"I'll see what I can do."

The next day is Kevin's party. Everything goes swimmingly. The cake ends up with eight candles on it, but nobody seems to mind and maybe by the time you get to 47 a shortage of candles is a bonus. My sister-in-law and I exchange knowing looks when Kevin opens his pool, which is Chinese, as expected. She threw in a surprise Chinese pump to inflate it.

"A pool!" Kevin exclaims. He turns to my sister-in-law. "How'd you guess?"

Kevin gives me a kiss after he opens the box with his $150 sunglasses from California. He tries them on and we all agree that he looks like a fighter pilot.

"*Sweetie,*" he says to me. And that's all he needs to say. He calls me

Sweetie all the time, even when he's annoyed with me, so it doesn't necessarily mean he's thrilled with me at any given moment. But this time when he says it he gives me a look that says all is forgiven. We all stay up late and chat over coffee and eat so much Betty Crocker white cake that our stomachs hurt. I haven't seen Kevin in this good a mood in weeks. He doesn't have to tell me, but I know instinctively that something else is in play. He's back on board for the boycott, at least for now.

I am not in the business of giving relationship advice, and I can't say what might work for others, but in our case all it took to restore matrimonial harmony was a cheap pool, expensive sunglasses, and a willingness to betray my convictions.

■ ■ ■

The Chinese girl on the cover of *Newsweek* (May 9, 2005) is drop-dead gorgeous and smiling like she's got the world by the tail, which, in many ways, she has.

"China's Century," declares the cover in banner letters above actress Ziyi Zhang's pretty head. The magazine tells me she is the face of new China. It's a very pretty face, with intelligent, shining eyes. If this is the face of new China, we have nothing to worry about.

I flip inside to the special report on China. It gets right to the point: China is big, and fascinating to Americans, but as it gains wealth and influence "the very size and scale that seemed so alluring is beginning to look ominous. And Americans are wondering whether the 'China threat' is nightmarishly real."

The story proceeds with a series of mind-bending statistics, all interesting, but I find they don't rattle me much. My worry over China has reached a saturation point. The boycott reminds me daily of China's deep reach into my life—into my former life, that is—and just in case I take the day off from worrying, inevitably some friend calls to relay some China-related news. This week, for instance, I am sitting at my computer and sweating a deadline when a friend calls to tell me how disappointed she is in the merchandise at Cost Plus World Market.

"They say World Market, but it seemed like almost everything in there is from China," she says. "They need to change the name to Cost Plus Chinese Market. You'd have a hard time shopping there."

I think about China on all manner of occasions. After reading a story in the newspaper about a series of home-invasion robberies in our neighborhood I decide we should get a "Beware of Dog" sign for our back gate, maybe one with a snarling Doberman on it, but I worry that we won't be able to find one from any place but China. I am pleasantly surprised when Kevin brings home a metal "Beware of Dog" sign made by a firm in Northfield, Ohio.

When Kevin takes a two-day trip to Cincinnati, he struggles to find souvenir toys for the kids. He buys T-shirts instead.

"I couldn't find anything else in the airport gift shop that wasn't from China," Kevin tells me, apologetic.

Wes doesn't hide his disappointment. When Kevin leaves the living room, Wes whispers in my ear.

"I was hoping for a car," he confesses.

I think about China during Wes's swimming lessons at the YMCA. After his first lesson he tells me the teacher wants to dunk him under the water when I'm not looking.

"He's not a good guy, Mama," he says.

"He's a nice young man," I insist. "And I won't let him dunk you. I'll jump in the pool and pull you out if I see your teacher try anything like that. But I promise he's not going to try it."

Wes looks unconvinced, so I try bribery. I tell him I'll buy him a kickboard like his cousin's and a pair of swim goggles if he'll continue with the lessons. He sees an opening.

"Can I have two kickboards?" he asks. "Two blue ones?"

At precisely that moment, some other mother, somewhere out in the universe, must have been having an out-of-body experience and decided to descend into my body to seize control of my vocal cords. I can't see any other explanation for what I hear my voice say next. It is something one of those appeasing mothers would say, the ones who end up feeding their children M&M's for breakfast and buying them every toy they see on television because they don't have the good sense to say no to their children. I am so very different from them, always have been. So it's quite astonishing to hear the voice—*my* voice—say, "Yes, you can have two."

I can't believe how weak I've become. Maybe I'm worn down from saying no too often. Or just worn out in general.

"What about two goggles?" Wes wants to know next.

I scrimp together leftover bits of backbone from an earlier era and hear myself say no.

I head to the store a few days later, hoping I haven't promised too much. My China instinct tells me kickboards are not Chinese, by virtue of the fact that they bear some resemblance to life-saving flotation devices, whose life-saving purpose bears some resemblance to medicine, and medicine is not something we trust the Chinese to make, or so I've noticed from reading the tubes and bottles stashed in cupboards around our house. The creation of furniture, toys, cell phones, shoes, stereos, and answering machines—these we trust to China. But pills to keep us well and things to keep our children from sinking to the bottom of the pool, somehow these don't fit the Chinese mold.

I'm wrong about the Chinese mold. The shelves of the pool-supplies aisle at Target are thick with Chinese flotation devices for babies. That seems to bode poorly for the prospect of a non-Chinese kickboard, but I get lucky again. I find a blue one with a fish on it and turn it over to check the label. *Made in Taiwan*, it says. I put a single kickboard into my shopping cart and hope that Wes's memory is not as good as his father's and that he won't remember that I agreed to provide two of them. My sister-in-law tipped me off about Canadian swim goggles on the same aisle; the search for an inflatable pool got her into label-reading mode. I snatch up a pair of Canadian goggles that look like lizard eyes and head for the cashier.

On the way out of the parking lot I pass the jewelry store where I bought my watch battery four months ago. I've got time to spare today and I should park the car, march in there, and clear up the matter of a possibly Chinese battery. But I find I don't have the stomach for it.

Soon, I tell myself, but not today.

■ ■ ■

I keep an eye on Mona Williams, or at least her name. Mona Williams is the main spokesperson for Wal-Mart, and since I thrill to deliciously negative stories about Wal-Mart, I frequently come across her name as she defends her employer from all manner of accusation and innuendo.

In the issue of *Newsweek* that arrives a week after the special China edition, Ms. Williams claims the magazine had it wrong when it reported that much of Wal-Mart's merchandise comes from China. In a letter to the editor, she says the retailer spent just $18 billion on Chinese goods in 2004, compared to $137.5 billion from U.S. suppliers. She says the Chinese purchases come to less than 6 percent of the American total. *Newsweek* runs an apology with her letter.

I read the letter again, then lean back on the sofa to think about it. Something about Ms. William's claims doesn't sit right with me. My gut tells me she's spinning me and other *Newsweek* readers by playing fast and loose with the numbers. I've got nothing to support my hunch except memories from the days when I shopped at Wal-Mart, and what I remember from those days is that you can't swing a cat in Wal-Mart without knocking over a pile of Chinese merchandise. It's conceivable that I've got it wrong. Perhaps I was always checking the labels on the wrong things in Wal-Mart, homing in on rare Chinese products in a store packed with goods made in New Hampshire and Tennessee. Yet somehow I don't think that's it. I see one way to find out.

There is a stir of excitement in my stomach the next day when I head for Wal-Mart. Wal-Mart has been a forbidden destination since I gave it up a couple of years ago, so it feels pleasantly devious to visit the place now. Going there under false pretenses adds to the thrill. To the casual observer, I resemble an ordinary Wal-Mart shopper looking for bargains on shampoo and macaroni and cheese, when in fact I'm here hoping to catch Wal-Mart in a fib. Maybe this is what it feels like to be Geraldo Rivera, busting open a scandal on network television with a hidden camera clipped to his lapel. Or maybe a spy.

My mission is simple: Examine 100 items for sale at Wal-Mart, record the name of the country where each is made, and then calculate the Chinese-versus-American ratio of merchandise. It's not science, but it will tell me something.

I sweep by the greeter, an old man with white hair wearing the traditional blue vest with the words "How May I Help You?" in white letters on the back. He's checking the receipts of a crowd of teenage girls to make sure they haven't helped themselves to a five-finger discount on lip gloss and eye liner. I am not sure where to start, but I spot racks of swimming suits straight ahead so I decide to begin there, then roam the store by whim. I open my notebook, stop next to a rack of ladies' suits, pick up one, and examine the label. I write down, "One-piece ladies swimsuit, Taiwan."

I work my way through the racks, making stops in socks and underwear, then accessories, and next the girls' department. I take a break after 10 minutes to chart my progress. I am taken aback to see that there is nothing from China among the first 14 items on my list. For a moment, I wonder whether Mona Williams wasn't sincere when she downplayed China's role in stocking Wal-Mart's shelves. I come to my senses. That can't be it. I've been to Wal-Mart and Wal-Mart sells tons of stuff from China, so there's got to be some other explanation. I get back to work.

The next item I examine is a 40DD Sweet Nothings bra in pale pink. *Made in China*, the label says. Aha. Now we're getting somewhere.

I head next to housewares, toys, then electronics, writing furiously as I move through the aisles and hoping nobody asks me what I'm doing. Things go smoothly until I stop before a bank of televisions, all Chinese, as far as I can see.

"Hey," a voice says. "What are you up to?"

I look up into the face of our old neighbor. Up to? How did he know I was *up to* anything? What kind of question is that? I feel my face go red. I fold my arms, tucking my notebook under one arm to hide it. He probably gives me a pass in the inexplicable behavior department, since we are transplants from California, and also because I am married to Kevin, who has a reputation for colorful antics among our neighbors, so maybe I should come clean with what I am up to. But his wife owns a local clothing store that sells a lot of Chinese merchandise—I've checked the labels—so I'd rather not tell him for fear of sounding high and mighty, or worse.

I adopt a casual tone.

"Oh, you know, looking at stuff," I say. "Getting a feel for things."

He studies me.

"Getting a feel for things at Wal-Mart?" he asks.

"Yes," I say. "Just checking where things come from."

I wave my hand toward the televisions.

"Maybe one day our television will break down and we'll need to get a new one. Now I'll know what's out here."

He doesn't appear to buy this, but he's too polite to pry further. He changes the subject and asks about the kids and Kevin. I ask about his wife and his daughters. Then, when I've made the minimally required amount of small talk, I make my excuses, jet out of electronics, and head for a section in the middle of the store that ought to be called General Miscellany.

I've been poking around General Miscellany for a few minutes when a Chinese ceramic Jesus stops me cold. The Jesus figurine shares shelf space with big-eyed clowns and porcelain kittens. I pick him up, confirm that he is indeed from China, and then hover in the aisle and study him in the bright lights. He looks melancholy, and he makes me feel the same. What I'd like to know is whether anybody bothers to explain who this guy is to the Chinese workers who crafted him. It seems only fair that if you are going to ask somebody to spend 14 hours a day painting Jesus figurines then you might mention the big picture to them, perhaps tell them his name, and even point out that he cuts quite a figure in religious circles around the globe.

There's some larger meaning at work here, but I can't pin it down. I wish my mother were here. She can cut to the heart of the matter like nobody's business when Jesus is involved. She would probably point out that we've got Jesus, famous defender of the poor, molded and painted by poor Chinese workers on the other side of the world, hauled across the globe in ships and trucks to eventually land here, alongside kittens and clowns, where he generates sales for the richest retailer in the world, and far from the kindest, no matter what Mona Williams might like me to believe. My mother would be indignant about Jesus's ignoble place on a shelf alongside figurines of questionable taste. She would see straight off that this ceramic Jesus is mixed up with all kinds of things, not the least of which is irony.

I'm half tempted to buy the Jesus figurine, to rescue him from his place on the shelf, but I've been up to no good breaking China-boycott rules with the inflatable pool, so at least I should stick to the Wal-Mart ban. I put Jesus back on the shelf and move down the aisle. I add a few more things to my list, then do a fast count of what I've got so far. My list has 106 items. I head for home.

When I get home I take out our calculator and run the numbers. It takes me about half an hour to sort out my list, but it's clear early on that China is in charge of the store's general merchandise: 52 of the items on the list, or 49 percent, were made there. The United States contributes 23 items, for a 22 percent share of the total. Honduras takes a distant third, accounting for four items. The rest of the merchandise comes from points around the globe as diverse as Italy (socks), Pakistan (underwear), and Turkey (a tank top).

My list suggests all kinds of things, including that Mona Williams has some explaining to do. I am not claiming victory over the Wal-Mart publicity machine—not yet, anyway. It's possible that Mona Williams' numbers will hold up somehow. Granted, I did not venture into the aisles of Wal-Mart where America rules—say pet food, groceries, and beauty products—but I also didn't spend much time in areas where China is in charge, like toys and electronics. The way I see it, unless Ms. Williams is including groceries, or building supplies used to construct Wal-Mart stores, in her tally of American purchases, I just don't see how her numbers add up.

My findings suggest other things. I notice that all the patriotic themed items—red, white, and blue bunting, an American flag, and cotton fabric with flags on it—are made in the USA. I suspect this is because Wal-Mart's savvy buyers know shoppers are feeling damp-eyed with love of country when they shop for bunting and flags, and are more inclined to check the country-of-origin labels than when they are looking for shoes or towels. Just a guess, but my feeling is you don't become the biggest company in the land without some understanding of your customers.

Other items inspire hazy musings about the global economy. Take Lesotho's contribution to the list, a jumbo Just My Size ladies' tank top. On one hand, you could see it as encouraging that a tiny African nation is doing business with Wal-Mart. In a certain light, that seems like progress. Lesotho has a toehold on the global economy, you might say. On the other hand, the idea that Wal-Mart relies on desperate workers in dirt-poor nations to turn out underwear at rock-bottom prices to boost revenues and score points with shareholders gets me churned up. Wal-Mart goes to Lesotho because Lesotho makes it worth Wal-Mart's while, and the only way Lesotho can make it worth Wal-Mart's while is by working for so little that Wal-Mart isn't tempted to go elsewhere. Lesotho's got everything to lose if this relationship turns bad. Lesotho's got no hand.

Next I consider what the petite Chinese ladies who stitched the 40DD Sweet Nothings bra think of the garment's super-size proportions. How do they envision the extra-large ladies who will wear the bras on the other side of the earth? Or do they think of them at all? I suppose it's too much to hope that the factory managers explain the ironic name on the packaging. Sweet Nothings—hardly.

I will never get answers to these questions, but there is one mystery that I may be able to clear up. A few weeks after my trip to the store I call Wal-Mart's corporate communications office in Bentonville, Arkansas. I explain to the lady who answers that I'd like to talk to someone about the company's use of overseas suppliers. I leave a message on voice mail for somebody named Bill Wertz.

He never calls me back.

I have practically built a sideline career for myself out of jumping to nasty conclusions about Wal-Mart. I see no reason not to jump to another one now. I've got Wal-Mart running scared.

■ ■ ■

My printer runs out of ink. Normally, this is not cause for alarm, but I get a sinking feeling when the machine halts without warning and tells me it's time for a new cartridge. I've been wrong before, but my developing China instinct tells me that China is in charge of ink cartridges in the current age.

I'm feeling blue later as I follow a woman to the printer section in the office supply store.

"This is it," she says. She hands me a box and walks away.

I turn over the box for the ritual inspection of the label. It's bad news, as expected. Toner made in Japan, it says. Cartridge made in China. The cartridge is the one that's supposed to fit my printer—the manufacturer warns of the dangers of using other brands—but I check the other brands on the shelf anyway, thinking maybe I'll find a non-Chinese one that will work for me. They are all Chinese. By the time I get home I am in the mood for kindness and sympathy. I don't get either one.

"Great," says Kevin, his voice oozing sarcasm. "Now we have a printer we can't use."

He gives me a disgusted look.

"Oh, but you're a writer, so I guess you won't need a printer much," he adds. "Good thing I spent $200 on that thing."

Guess who's feeling grouchy about the boycott again?

CHAPTER

SIX

Mothers of Invention

On a trip to the craft store I learn two things about the Fourth of July: that it begins in February, and that it is just as Chinese as Christmas.

I stop to gawk at the rows of red, white, and blue merchandise as soon as I step inside the store entrance. It's a staggering display. July 4th-themed dolls, tricolor icicle lights, coffee mugs, flower pots, door wreaths, vases, cookie jars, ceramic animals, candle holders, tablecloths, and American flags teeter precariously on shelves that reach 12 feet toward the white-tiled ceiling above me.

On this particular afternoon, patriotism is available at bargain prices; signs taped to the shelves at eye level declare the merchandise 50 percent off. I stand and soak it in. Later, when I find an assistant manager she informs me, when I ask, that the July 4th merchandise hits the shelves just after Valentine's Day. I was in here a few weeks ago but don't remember any of this. I don't know how I could have missed it.

"We put July 4th out with Easter," the assistant manager explains. "And then after Easter it's just July 4th."

"Until when?" I ask.

"Until it's time for the Christmas items," she answers.

"And when does the Christmas merchandise go out?"

"July."

"Do people really shop for July 4th in February and Christmas in July? Are they really in the mood?"

"Oh, yes," she says, smiling. "The merchandise moves."

I head back to the July 4th section to take a closer look. I expect a Chinese blowout and for the most part I get it, though there are exceptions. There are napkin holders from the Philippines, oversize bows and plastic glow sticks from Mexico, and Taiwanese stencils that allow you to write "USA" in sugar crystals on the tops of frosted cupcakes. I find two American-made items: a felt flag kit and a July 4th welcome mat. Nevertheless, it's clear from the get-go that China's in charge of decorations for the nation's birthday, and often contributes an ironic sentiment to the occasion. A wooden Chinese wind chime beckons me to "Let Freedom Ring" in hand-painted lettering. On the same shelf I find a Chinese vase with the words "United We Stand" on it and a curving set of Chinese lights that spell "God Bless America." There are Chinese Uncle Sam tablecloths and Chinese July 4th metal angels that undoubtedly started out as Chinese Christmas angels until they were hastily dabbed with red, white, and blue paint in an effort to clear unsold inventory from some distant factory floor.

I discover where you buy the ribbon-shaped bumper magnets that say "Support Our Troops" and "Never Forget, September 11, 2001." You buy them at the craft superstore, which buys them from China.

As with the ceramic Jesus at Wal-Mart, I wonder if anybody bothers to translate for the Chinese workers the meaning of the words on the magnets, or explains why somebody half a world away would want to buy one and stick it on the bumper of their car.

As I linger in the aisles, it occurs to me that almost nobody I know dresses up the house for July 4th, which suggests that I know either the

right people or the wrong ones. I can't remember the last time I went
to a party with bunting on the fence. I can say with conviction that I've
never entered a home with a July 4th metal angel on display. Our own
observance of the holiday is low-key, though often loud. Kevin likes
fireworks for the 4th, but I've put the kibosh on his pyrotechnics since
the arrival of the children, and he turns up his nose at my suggestion of
sparklers as a too-tame alternative. This year it will be me turning up a
nose at sparklers, since I'd wager good money they are made in China.
Naturally, I worry that Kevin will take a sudden interest in sparklers
now that they are off-limits.

I try to get into the spirit of things. I buy two packages of Mexican
red and blue glow sticks for the children and head out into the heat. As
I walk to the car I make a mental note to return in July to check out
the Christmas merchandise. I also kick myself for neglecting to buy art
supplies, which is what brought me to the craft store in the first place.
I kick myself for something else, too. I forgot to ask the assistant manager an obvious question: If the Christmas inventory goes out after July
4th, when do they put Halloween and Thanksgiving merchandise on
the shelves?

■ ■ ■

At work my boss points out that I'm fooling myself if I think I've been
avoiding Chinese products, despite what product labels tell me.

"Chinese components are everywhere," he says. "You can't avoid
those, no matter how hard you try. It's impossible."

It's a point I've been ruminating for months, ever since I kept the
American lamp with the Chinese part in it. This week I was reminded
again of the difficulty of avoiding China when I purchased earrings
from a local artist. I was feeling pleased with myself until I got home
and noticed the free gift box they came in was made in China.

My boss continues his critique.

"You know what you are doing? You are delaying your dependence
on China, not escaping it," he says. "You're also kidding yourself."

This is my *nice* boss talking. *His* boss, a frequent grouch, didn't slow down when I tried to stop him to suggest that I write a series of stories on the boycott for the business magazine where I work.

"Nobody gives a crap about that stuff but you," he tossed over his shoulder. "Sounds like another one of your ploys to slam Wal-Mart."

I suspect the nice boss has been spending too much time with the grouchy one, because they are starting to sound a lot alike.

"Maybe you can make it a year without Chinese products, but sooner or later you'll be eating from China's hand," the nice boss says. "There's no getting around it."

I sneer at him as he turns to leave.

"Thanks for your support," I say to his back.

He's right, of course, which makes him all the more irritating. I'm not living normally without Chinese items. I'm coming up with stopgap measures to tide me over until I've got other options, presumably Chinese ones. Take the printer cartridge. After it ran dry I began asking Kevin to print pages for me on his office printer, which itself is quite possibly Chinese; I never dared to ask him to pull it from the wall and check the label on the back for me. He was grumpy enough about printing the pages and I didn't want to push my luck.

Then Kevin left town—he's off to Paris, to run a summer study-abroad program for the university—putting an end to that option. Since then I've been sending documents to myself at work by e-mail, then printing them out there. It's only a few pages and a little ink but I bring American copy paper from home to ease my guilt over conducting personal business at work. I keep reminding myself to take a look at the back of the office printer, and also the cartridge inside it, to pin down where they were made, for the record, but I'm afraid one of my co-workers will see me and ask what I'm up to. I'd probably make a full confession, and then maybe they'd tell the grumpy boss, who might fire me for using company ink. Or worse—he would let me keep my job but tell me I couldn't print at work any more. Then I'd really be in a jam. I'd have to drive to the public library, which lets you print 20 pages for free during each visit. I checked the other day, in case it comes to that.

Our inkless printer is one of a series of recent troubles in the area of electronics, where China is king. One day, lying on the sofa, I tick them off in my head.

One: The screen of our little television has started to go dark for minutes at a time, including at least twice during the climax of a public-television mystery when we were on the edge of our seats.

Two: The CD player stopped working after Sofie stuck something inside the disc tray when I wasn't looking. I don't know what her weapon is, but it's small and deadly, at least to the CD player, which now makes endless clicks every time I turn it on, but no music. Every day or two, I press the power button to see if the problem has resolved itself, but so far no dice. I'm not the only one who misses listening to music, either. On torrid afternoons, when it's too hot to venture outside, I let the children pull the cushions off the sofa and blast a Muppets version of "Jingle Bell Rock" over and over while they jump on the springs of the sofa. These days they bounce in silence. Without music their bouncing has a joylessness that reminds me of the overweight ladies I've seen dutifully executing movements in water-aerobics class at the YMCA near our house. Nobody looks like they are having much fun.

Three: Adult fun is likewise in jeopardy these days. The blade on our blender broke the other day, and when I called the manufacturer they told me the replacement blades they sell are made in China.

"So you're telling me we can't make margaritas this summer?" Kevin asks me during a call home from France. Paris is supposed to make people feel romantic. I can hear something in his voice but it doesn't sound like love.

Four: The vacuum has stopped sucking, despite my vigorously cleaning its ghastly insides. I suspect whatever is blocking it has something to do with China. Perhaps I suctioned up an old toy.

In short, when I look around the house these days I see a series of problems, almost all of them with Chinese solutions.

I should be really worked up about all of this, but malaise has taken over, a function of humid days in the 90s. There on the sofa, I stare at the ceiling and consider the worst-case scenario. If I can't find anything but Chinese replacements for the jammed stereo, the erratic television, the bladeless blender, and the powerless vacuum cleaner, I can live with that. I can live without all of those things, at least for now, maybe forever. In some ways it will be a relief to get rid of them; as always, the house seems overly full of *things* that need to be dusted and arranged and repaired. I like to think that I am secretly a minimalist when it comes to material possessions. This could be my chance to find out if I mean it.

In any case, these are not problems without solutions, even with the limits imposed by the boycott. I can read books instead of watching mind-rotting television, for instance. The children are almost assured of becoming brilliant if I deprive them of the tube and read to them instead. The lack of a working stereo is equally unproblematic. We can listen to music while we are in the car. At home, the children can continue to destroy the springs of the sofa with silent bouncing. They may not be having as much fun as they did when "Jingle Bell Rock" rattled the walls, but technically they are not being harmed, either. The broken vacuum is the least of my worries. I can sweep the floors, a time-saver, really, since I'd be getting a workout in the process of cleaning the house. And margaritas can be made on the rocks.

The year is nearly half over. I can survive without all these things. Most of the world survives without them every day. It's only in my spoiled American reality that life without these things becomes in any way problematic. Honestly, how hard could it be to live without a television, a stereo, a vacuum cleaner, or a blender? Not too hard, I conclude. Then I think that maybe that's not the right question. A better question might be: How hard would it be to live with Kevin without these things?

■ ■ ■

Like his father, Wes sees little virtue in a China boycott.

"Do we not like China?" he asks me one day.

I am alarmed by the question.

"Yes, we like China," I tell him.

He presses on.

"Are they not nice to people?"

"They are perfectly good people in China," I assure him. "No different than people anywhere else."

"Then how come we don't buy China things?" he asks.

We've been over this territory before but I stumble every time. Many days I can't quite remember myself why we are doing this, so to explain it in a way that makes sense to a four-year-old is beyond my abilities. Still, I suppose it's my duty to try.

"We like China, but it's a very big place, with lots of factories, and we want to give other countries a chance to sell us things," I say.

He looks at me in silence, nose scrunched up and eyes squinty, fingers squeezed hard around his peanut butter sandwich. For a moment I imagine that I have pushed aside the haze of his tender understanding of the world. I picture a thought bubble above his little head. "Oh, I see," it says inside the bubble, "a fairer world, where everybody gets to do a little business, and oversized steamrollers, like China and America, don't smash everybody up."

Wes brings me back to earth.

"Do light swords come from China?" he asks. "Tyler has a light sword. I want one for Christmas. I know Santa is going to bring me one."

I look at him in silence. I don't have the heart to tell him that light swords come from China. I haven't checked for sure, but by this point I don't have to. And who knows? The Christmas shopping season is months away. Maybe by then a factory in Vietnam or Cambodia will start turning out light swords and shipping them to wholesale toy distributors in places like Texas and California and they will eventually end up on store shelves in our neighborhood. I realize the odds are long, but it could happen. Stranger things have.

"Put it on your list for Santa," I tell Wes. "We'll see what he thinks. But keep in mind that the list to Santa is only a *suggestion* list. There's no such thing as a sure bet at Christmas."

Wes pauses over his sandwich. His eyes reproach me for my scant faith in the magic of Christmas.

"But Mama," he says, "I know Santa is going to get me one."

■ ■ ■

A mouse has moved in under the kitchen sink, a development that at first seems unconnected to the China boycott. My mother, who is visiting from California, is the first to spot it. The mouse leaps out of the trash can and skitters into the darkness after she opens the cupboard to throw something away. She slams the door shut and spends the afternoon with a nervous eye in that direction.

"I got a good look," she tells me. "There was no mistaking it for something else."

It could be worse—it could be a rat—but the news isn't good. Kevin isn't due back from France for two weeks. I will have to deal with the mouse myself. I am filled with dread at the thought of what lies ahead. There is even a slight feeling of betrayal. Ours is in many ways a traditional marriage. I send the Christmas cards, remember birthdays, and choose the paint colors. Kevin works the barbeque, sweats over blocked pipes, and deals with vermin and anything dead lodged under the house. This division of matrimonial duties is instinctive and unspoken. Pest control falls clearly within the bounds of Kevin's obligations, yet he is thousands of miles and two weeks away from the kitchen cupboard and the mouse within. I have no choice. I will tackle Kevin's job and deal with the intruder.

Or will I? I am gripped by a sense of urgency when my mother first tells me about the mouse, but then it occurs to me that maybe it was a one-time occurrence, never to be repeated. Maybe my mother gave that mouse such a fright when she slammed the cupboard door that it fled the premises for good in search of safer terrain. Or maybe I can keep the house so clean that there's nothing to keep it hanging around here. If I put every speck of food in the refrigerator and tackle the floors with broom and mop like my life depended on it, maybe I can deprive the mouse of so much as a stale, forgotten Cheerio to sustain it. I haven't heard of these methods working for others, but you never know. And maybe the situation isn't as urgent as it seems. If I put my mind to it, perhaps I could live with a mouse in the house for two weeks, if the mouse is reasonable and stays out of my way. We could each pretend we didn't know about the other and carry on until Kevin gets back and takes charge of the situation.

The trouble is, this mouse doesn't keep to itself. It has no tact whatever. The day after my mother sees it, it leaves distasteful evidence of its visits in the laundry room and on the kitchen counter, next to my checkbook and a stack of clean laundry. The day after that I discover that it has spent time in the downstairs crib, giving me chills and conjuring fears of hantavirus. Next it devours a pack of Juicy Fruit gum inside my mother's purse, then uses her purse as a bathroom. My mother is due to return to California in a few days. I can't help but notice that this time she seems eager to go.

I start to think that ignoring the mouse is not actually a solution to the problem.

"Don't kill it," Kevin commands me over the phone.

It's late at night in Paris, where Kevin is enjoying summer air drifting in through the open window of his clean, mouseless hotel room. We've been weighing my options for mouse disposal. We've ruled out poison—seems dangerous since we have children and a dog, plus there's the unpleasant business of the mouse dying within our walls. I confess I'm intimidated by the idea of an old-fashioned wooden snapping trap. I worry about my fingers, and, of course, there would be the aftermath of dealing with the dead mouse. I am squeamish about skittering things but I am more squeamish still about dead ones. Kevin pushes for a sentimental solution. He directs me to purchase one of the humane mousetraps we used in our old house, little plastic boxes that swing shut when the mouse ventures inside.

"The kids would love it if you caught it and let it go someplace," he says. "You could let it go down by the lake by the rich people's houses. It would be a great family project. That's what you should do."

No, that's what *you* should do, I think, but I keep quiet.

I stall for a day or two, until my neighbor points out something I hadn't considered.

"Maybe the mouse is pregnant and about to have babies," she says. "You'd never get rid of them all after that."

I head for the hardware store that afternoon. That's when the boycott gets in the way of a kinder, gentler means of mouse elimination. A sober young man leads me to the pest-control aisle after I ask if they sell humane mousetraps. I sense trouble as soon as I read the label on the outside of the trap. *Made in China*, it says.

I turn to the young man. He has dark, judging eyes, but I decide to let him in on my dilemma anyway. I've noticed that my sheepishness in admitting what I'm up to with the boycott declines in inverse measure to my level of desperation.

"Do you carry any other brands of humane traps?" I ask him. I hold up the trap for his inspection.

"You see, it says here that it's made in China, but I don't buy Chinese products," I explain.

The young man narrows his dark eyes, then turns gravely to study the shelves of traps before us. He reaches for a traditional wood-and-wire trap made by the Victor company and turns the package in his hand until he locates the product label.

"This one says made in the USA, but that could be just the plastic bag that holds it, not the trap inside," he tells me solemnly. "But it may be your best option."

This kid's got a knack for a China boycott. Nothing slips past him, I can tell. I shrug and hold out my hand.

"I'll take two," I say.

I don't set the American traps. To tell you the truth, I wasn't certain I was game to do it when I bought them, and not just because I fear for the well-being of my fingers. I don't set the traps because I continue to hope that the mouse will disappear of its own accord and I won't have to deal with it for the simple, irrational reason that I don't *want* to deal with it. Then I think I get lucky. One morning I smell death in the laundry room. Normally, I'd be horrified to think that something had died inside our house, but if the mouse can make its exit without my assistance I'm all for it. I am capable of avoiding the laundry room for a few days. I am in a fine mood when I leave for work in the morning, thinking I've dodged another bullet, but when I return in the afternoon my hopes are dashed. The odor has dissipated. It wasn't mouse death after all, merely a load of damp towels in the dryer.

I check the calendar in the kitchen. A little over a week remains until Kevin's return. I leave the traps unopened in the plastic bag from the hardware store and hope for the best—and, for the mouse, the worst.

■ ■ ■

I set aside thoughts of mice and set about patching up the household. I take the vacuum cleaner to a repair shop on the outskirts of town, where the owner waxes philosophical on a growing divide in the world of vacuum cleaners. More and more, you've got two choices in vacuums, he tells me. Cheap Chinese ones that will fall apart in a couple of years, or slick German jobs that start at $400 and run to $1,000 or more.

"I've got nothing in between," he says.

He clears out the hose of our machine for free and sends me on my way in 10 minutes' time.

"Come back in a couple of years when this one breaks," he calls as I'm on my way out the door. I take with me a brochure advertising German vacuum cleaners.

The television apparently heals itself. The screen hasn't gone dark in a couple of weeks. I consider the matter closed. Over the phone, Kevin tells me he will take the DVD player to a repair shop near our house when he gets back from France.

"The guy there is some kind of genius when it comes to fixing stuff," he says. "He'll figure it out, no problem."

I come up short in finding a fix only for the blender. I move it onto a shelf in the laundry room for the time being—careful to make sure the coast is clear, mouse-wise, when I open the cupboard—in the hope that Kevin won't ask about it upon his return.

■ ■ ■

No sooner have I cleared up my electronics problems than I run into new sunglasses trouble. The delicate metal filigree on my old Italian sunglasses is coming apart. A lens pops out of the thin plastic wire that holds it in place. I retrieve one of the flimsy Chinese pairs that came from Kevin's department secretary, but a day or two later I drop it on the concrete floor of the bathroom during a field trip to the zoo with Wes's preschool class. The glasses break decisively into two pieces on the floor. I recover the pieces and drop them in the overflowing trash can, a fitting exit to their brief, unsatisfactory appearance in our lives.

I find a low-tech solution to the lack of sunglasses: squinting.

To stay positive, I try not to think of three things: the useless printer, the broken drawer in the kitchen, and the fact that we've just run out of Chinese staples.

■ ■ ■

"It's considered a rude question," Kevin tells me over the phone.

"Then how do people in Europe know where the things they buy come from?" I ask him.

"Apparently, for the most part, they don't," he says. "Unless they ask, and, like I said, that's generally considered impolite. I get a lot of funny looks when I ask that."

In the days before Kevin left for France I realized that his time abroad might serve a handy purpose. He could load up on toys and trinkets made in France to give us a leg up on the looming Christmas holiday. This is sneaky and seems to run counter to the spirit of the boycott, but I'm really worried about Christmas and, technically, there is nothing in the boycott rules to prevent it. It turns out my sneaky idea is a loser. Kevin has been striking out as he visits the shops and markets of Paris in search of goods made in France.

He recounts his efforts so far. One day he is about to pay for three Eiffel Tower key chains from a man at a street market when he remembers to ask the man where they were made.

"En Chine," the man replies. In China.

Kevin dutifully holds them out to the man to return them.

"When I explained to the guy why I couldn't buy them, he was really understanding," he tells me. "He asked me where I was from and then told me it's because of Chinese imports and thirty years of bad French government that the only way he can make a living is selling things on the black market."

Kevin encounters other kindred spirits among the French. When he goes to a menswear shop to order a suit and asks where they are made, the girl tells him more and more customers are asking the same question. She tells Kevin about the customer who tried on a pair of pants but then decided against buying them because they were made in China.

Mostly he gets blank, even hostile, looks.

"The clerk at the grocery store walked away from me without answering when I asked where a T-shirt was made," he says. "I think he considered it harassment."

He assures me he will continue to scout for French gifts, despite hostile clerks.

"I'll be honest with you," he cautions. "France is pretty Chinese, too."

■ ■ ■

Meanwhile, the mouse lays low before resurfacing, bolder than before.

I'm sitting at the kitchen table, going through the mail, when I hear the rustling of a plastic bag under the sink, the precise spot where my mother first met the mouse. I have moved the trash bag to the outside of the cupboard, where it hangs from a drawer pull, to keep it out of the mouse's reach and to avoid my having to open the cupboard door for fear of what I might find inside. The trash can still has a plastic bag in it, although, as the mouse will soon discover, it is empty.

I get up and tiptoe toward the cupboard. Along the way I grab a dish towel off the back of a chair—a weapon strikes me as a good idea—and motion to our dog Rick to stick close behind me. Rick gives me a bored look, exhales, and drops his head back to the floor.

I'm not typically a quick study, but this time I cobble together a plan to deal with the mouse in the few seconds it takes for me to travel the eight or nine feet from my chair to the cupboard door. I envision the scene unfolding like this: I will open the door, slowly pull the trash can toward me, and then throw the towel over the mouse to disorient it. Then I will grab the trash can, rush toward the back door, throw it open, and heave the whole business out into the backyard, producing such a harrowing experience for the mouse that it will flee the premises and never return.

I execute step one as planned and nudge open the door. Next I cautiously grip the rim of the can and ease it toward me, the towel clutched in my free hand. I peer over the edge into the interior of the white plastic bag within, every fiber of my body ready to spring into action.

It's a false alarm. When I look inside the can, there is nothing but empty plastic. The mouse has vanished without a trace. I sigh, straighten up, and retreat to the kitchen table, where I sit and consider my options, which are grim and few. I turn to look at the wall calendar. Five days until Kevin's return.

Next I take a long look at the dog, still splayed on the floor across the room. Rick is proving as useless as a dish towel as a form of anti-mouse weaponry, which is a shame, because since my mother left town the dog is the closest thing I've got to an adult companion to advise me on the boycott and other household calamities.

I try to suppress a rising bitterness against Kevin about my having to turn to a large, disinterested dog for comfort in a difficult time.

"Five days," I tell Rick, as he briefly opens an eye.

We'll never make it.

CHAPTER
SEVEN

Summer of Discontent

The children are manic with anticipation on the evening of Kevin's return from France. Sofie runs a blue streak around the kitchen table until she collides with a chair and dents her forehead. Wes puts too much vigor into jumping on the sofa springs and goes flying over an upholstered arm onto the stereo, somehow escaping injury. I mix up Kevin's flight information and leave him stranded at the airport for an hour until my older brother can rescue him.

By the time Kevin appears in the front door it's past the children's bedtime and their cheeks are streaked with tears. I'm not feeling so hot myself. But it's nothing an armful of European presents can't fix. Kevin opens a bag and doles out gift after gift: a French sailboat and a real knife for Wes (I frown but save my motherly intercession for later) and a French plush rabbit for Sofie. There are German wind-up toys, Italian underwear for me, and a stack of French chocolate bars for the mouse.

The chocolate is not intended for the mouse, but that's what chews its way through half a dozen gold-foiled bars on Kevin's first night home after we leave them unopened on a table in the living room. The fate of the chocolate has a transforming effect on Kevin's feelings about lethal pest control.

"Where did you say you put those wooden traps?" he asks the next morning as we survey the foil wrappers and slivers of uneaten chocolate littered across the floor.

To my surprise, I am not certain I want to tell him. I have had a change of heart on the subject of mouse murder in recent days. It's not that I completely object to the idea, but I find that I want one more chance to rid the place of the mouse without having to choose between two distasteful alternatives: violating the boycott with the purchase of a humane Chinese trap and sparing the mouse, or killing the mouse with a lethal American trap and sparing the boycott. This shift in sentiment arises from the fact that I have had my first face-to-face encounter with the mouse, which my mother rightly described to me, after her own meeting with it, as "a pretty little thing, if also filthy, and possibly diseased."

My meeting with the mouse takes place one afternoon when I am again sitting at the kitchen table and once more I hear the crinkle of a thin plastic grocery bag. As before, I slip out of my chair and begin a slow creep toward the cupboard below the sink, dish towel again poised at the ready. Then the mouse surprises me. Before I reach the cupboard, it leaps out of the plastic trash bag that I'd hung on a knob on the outside of the cupboard, runs in a pale flash along the top rim of the cupboard door, and disappears into a dark space between the cupboard and the trash compacter. I assumed I had removed the trash bag from the mouse's reach, but now it occurs to me that, if anything, I have made it more convenient for it to jump into the bag for a quick lunch and then make a hurried exit at the first hint of trouble. I made a fundamental mistake. I had considered the cupboard from my enormous human perspective rather than from the vantage point of the mouse, for which the narrow cupboard top is a wide swath of highway ideal for a quick getaway.

Mice are not smart animals, but I cede a grudging respect at being outwitted in this manner. And my mother was correct in her assessment of the mouse: cute, if also filthy. Yet I am as surprised as Kevin to hear myself voice objections to a fatal remedy on the morning after the mouse's chocolate binge.

"I've got an idea for a catch–and–release trap," I tell him. "Give me two nights to try it out."

He looks skeptical.

"Suit yourself," he says. "But on day three I'm getting down to business."

■ ■ ■

By now I know a thing or two about this mouse, which is why I feel optimistic that my idea for a homemade mousetrap will work. It plays on the mouse's known weaknesses: French chocolate, cookies, and a tendency to loiter in the vicinity of the kitchen sink.

That night, after the children are in bed, I funnel broken cookies and bits of chocolate into an empty milk jug. I place the jug on its side on the tiled counter next to the sink. Next I take a small, unopened can of tuna and place it below the opening of the jug as a makeshift stepping stool to help the mouse climb inside the jug. Then I hit the lights, head for bed, and wait for the sound of wobbling plastic, or maybe cookies being chewed by a tiny jaw. My trap is weak when it comes to an alarm mechanism, but our bedroom is adjacent to the kitchen and I feel certain that I will hear something to alert me to the mouse's capture. When I do, I will rise without sound, slip silently into the kitchen, grab the jug with the mouse inside, quickly turn it upright, and then plug the opening with the dish towel before it knows what's hit it. The next day we will drive to the lake and release the mouse near the rich people's houses, as Kevin has suggested. It will stagger off into the weeds, grateful for our mercy and groggy on too much sugar. End of mouse. End of story. Another winning episode in our battle to overcome the limits imposed on our lives by the China boycott.

I don't see how I can miss with this one.

Twice that night, scratching noises wake me and I rise to tiptoe into the kitchen. Twice I am disappointed when I grab the jug, plug the hole with the towel, flip on the lights, and learn that I have trapped only chocolate and cookies inside.

It's the same story on the second night: wake, creep, cap the jug, sag with disappointment.

On the third morning Kevin looks sternly at me over his mug of coffee.

"It's time to get serious," he says.

I am taken aback by Kevin's resolve. I thought he'd have yet another change of heart and start pushing again for a humane Chinese trap. I know him to have a soft spot for wild creatures, although whether a suburban mouse qualifies as wild is open for debate. Kevin likes to watch birds; he can tell you the difference between a nuthatch and a gnatcatcher. He captures spiders in the house in paper towels and shakes them free in the backyard. The year he lived in Alaska as a teenager his tender feelings for wild animals even threatened his and his older brother's winter survival plan. After the carnival where they worked closed for the season, the boys moved to an abandoned wilderness cabin nine miles from the village of Kasilof. They figured they could survive the snowy months on Tang, cornmeal mush, and whatever they could shoot. The plan fell apart when Kevin could not bring himself to pull the trigger on the .22 revolver even when a flock of plump ground fowl gathered to peck in the dirt around his feet.

"It was too easy to shoot something too dumb to be scared," he told me years later.

The brothers moved back to Anchorage, where Kevin sold stuffed animals and Christmas trees. His brother got a job at a loading dock, a position that required him to trudge seven miles through the snow each morning. They returned to California in the spring with hands untainted by the blood of Alaskan wildlife.

All of which is to say that I learn something about human nature, or

Kevin's nature, on this July morning three decades later. I learn that the passing of 30 years, the pride of home ownership, and the devastation of a stack of expensive French chocolate bars by an aggressive mouse can change a lot of things about a man, including his sentimental feelings toward members of the animal kingdom.

"The traps, please," Kevin repeats over his cup.

I point to the door of the laundry room.

"In there," I say. "Watch your fingers."

Kevin snares the mouse on the first go-round after setting the killer American trap under the sink, which is why I am so surprised to discover the mouse running along the floorboard of the laundry room a couple of days later. No wonder it covered so much turf in the days before Kevin's return. It had friends, or maybe relatives.

Kevin returns to the hardware store and loads up on American traps. We catch three more mice that week.

"That should do it," he says, one morning, after checking under the sink. "I think we're out of the mouse business."

His optimism seems premature, but I don't say anything. Kevin is rolling with the boycott's punches these days and I don't want to spoil his good mood. Since his return from France he has set about fixing up the household with cheerful pragmatism. Boycott-related complications do nothing to derail his sunny disposition. He drops off the jammed CD player at a local repair shop with instructions to the owner not to fix it if he has to use Chinese parts to get it working again. The owner assures him that "we get all our parts here locally, not from China."

Kevin doesn't press the issue with the man.

"I didn't want to mention that the store where you buy parts doesn't really have anything to do with where they are made," he says. "I didn't want to hurt his feelings."

Kevin rigs an old set of metal rabbit ears on top of the television to improve the picture. He doesn't mention the broken blender, the broken printer, or the lack of staples, which he hasn't yet discovered. He's given up his battle with the stuck kitchen drawer; I haven't caught him tugging on the handle even once in the days since he's been home. I worry that maybe we have hit a wall when we run out of glue and discover Elmer's is made in China, but Kevin runs around town without complaint until he locates a glue stick from Canada.

I suspect the good times won't last long, but I decide to enjoy them while they do.

■ ■ ■

I don't claim special powers of mental telepathy. Perhaps I should.

I read an ominous news story about the fate of the Lego Group of Denmark, which is losing money as sales of its plastic blocks plummet, apparently in part because modern children find them boring in comparison to flashing electronic toys. A Canadian competitor is also cutting into its business. Analysts speculate that the Danish firm will move much or even all of its production to cheaper overseas manufacturing sites, possibly in Asia, which I conclude means China. The townspeople of Billund, Denmark, are dyspeptic. Legos made them rich. Now Chinese Legos may make them poor.

I realize that it's not polite to blow your own horn, but I have to say I saw this one coming. I saw it three months ago, in the toy aisle at Target, on the label on a Lego box. I remember what it told me: parts made in Denmark and China. I felt a surge of panic, for myself and for Denmark. It seemed to me then that the writing was on the wall. I was unnerved by the idea that the company would run to China and never look back. I feel bad for Billund, but its townspeople can't blame me. Wes has started to complain that we buy *too many* Legos. They have become the default gift for birthday parties by virtue of the fact that we're locked out of the rest of the overwhelmingly Chinese toy market. I also happen to think that they make a fine gift, though lately Wes is having doubts.

"Can't we get something besides Legos?" he asks me one day. "We always buy Legos."

I can think of only one thing to tell him.

"No," I say.

■ ■ ■

"I've become a what?" I ask my friend.

"A source of controversy," he repeats into the phone. I can tell he's enjoying this.

"How's that?"

He says that he and his wife have been fielding calls from other parents in the neighborhood who are worried about whether they can bring Chinese gifts to Sofie's two-year-old birthday party.

"They think they will get in trouble if they bring a toy made in China, but they say that's all that's out there so they don't know what they are supposed to do," he says. "I told them they could bring what they wanted and you wouldn't get mad. I assured them ya'll aren't nut cases."

The way he says the last bit suggests the point is still up for discussion.

Sofie's party takes place a couple of days later. It is a chaotic affair that begins in our backyard in sweltering heat until a sudden rainstorm chases everyone inside the house, where the guests huddle over sagging paper plates of hot dogs and mist up the windows with damp bodies and breathing. By noon, half of the children are crying, including the birthday girl, who throws herself onto the ground and refuses to get up. One by one the guests drift out the front door into the wet midday heat.

When everybody has gone home and the house is quiet I inspect Sofie's gifts. Whatever my friend told the other parents must have reassured them that they should feel free to bring Chinese merchandise. There is a T-shirt from Nepal, a book from Singapore, and sunglasses from Taiwan, but China claims its traditional place as ruler of American children's birthday parties. China contributes two dolls, a stuffed dog, a toy purse, a backpack that looks like a bee, a puzzle, a Mr. Potato Head game, and a miniature horse farm.

It's nobody's fault, and I realize no boycott rules were broken, but I can't help but feel disappointed every time something Chinese enters the house. Undoubtedly, the gift exemption saved us from offending many people, starting with my mother, but I wonder now whether it was too liberal a loophole. It hadn't occurred to me how many gifts we receive, or that so many of them are made in China. It's too late to change the rule now, and while it may be regrettable, what's sorrier still is that I catch myself complaining for even a moment that we have so many friends and relatives eager to bestow us with gifts, albeit Chinese ones.

I console myself with small things. I tell myself that we did our best to keep China from attending Sofie's party. We put squat Italian tea lights on her cake rather than standard Chinese birthday candles. They weren't as festive as traditional candles, but I didn't dare ask my sister-in-law for help in the candle department so soon after Kevin's birthday. The Scooby-Doo cake decorations were made in France. The cake itself, the pink frosting on top of it, and the hot dogs were made in America. It's traditional to send the children home with party bags of small trinkets, but I find the bags are invariably filled with Chinese items. I skipped the gift bags and hoped no one would condemn us for being spoilsports or cheapskates.

■ ■ ■

Kevin's rebel streak resurfaces shortly before we leave on a trip to our hometown of San Diego, California. He comes home with several items to entertain the children during the three-hour plane ride, including a package of foam stickers shaped like fish. I turn over the package and frown at the label, then confront him with what I find.

"Do you realize these stickers are Chinese?" I ask. "Did you even check the label?"

He smiles grimly at me. Something in his body language informs me I'm back on shaky ground with Kevin. His look dares me to suggest that he drive back to the store to return the stickers. An inner voice tells me not to take the bait, but I can't resist a mild rebuke.

"You do realize that I'm going to have to write this down," I tell him. "For the record. It's a clear violation of the boycott. I have to tell you I'm surprised you haven't got the hang of things by now."

He bobs his head and pulls down the corners of the mouth, making it clear that it would be a metaphysical impossibility for him to care less about the matter of the Chinese stickers.

"Well," I say. "Just so you know."

The boycott trails us to California. Kevin packs his bad attitude for the trip.

"The kids need squirt guns," he announces on our first morning in my mother's house. "Wes needs sunglasses."

He gestures impatiently to his feet, which are clad in a pair of aging running shoes.

"And I need flip-flops. All the ones at the drugstore were Chinese, but just so you know I'm not wearing shoes and socks to the beach."

My mother is also playing hardball these days.

"Does it bother you to touch those?" she sneers one evening while I'm making pesto with Chinese pine nuts. "I wouldn't want you to sully your hands."

Even the children's godmother, as good-natured a soul as ever walked the earth, can't resist a jab when we arrive at her house for a barbeque.

"Don't worry," she says as she hands me a colorful bag containing a belated birthday gift for Sofie. "None of it's from China."

Inside the bag are Vietnamese tennis shoes, a Turkish skirt, and an Indonesian bathing suit. We've been friends for 20 years but I didn't re-alize, until now, that she was capable of sarcasm. I am a little hurt and object to her suggestion that I am somehow being difficult.

"You know you don't have to boycott China," I tell her. "That's just the rule for us."

"Are you kidding?" she responds, eyes wide. "I'm not ruining your experiment."

I don't mention that Kevin is already busy doing that, and I'm not far behind him. A China boycott can be a lonely business.

■ ■ ■

My family isn't finished picking at me when I read a news story that gets me picking away at myself. A piece in the *Los Angeles Times* describes an elderly Chinese couple who have taken in more than 40 abandoned children over the years. The husband, 82, makes his living as a scavenger; his wife, 81, spends her days at home caring for the children, many of whom have disabilities. They took in their first baby when they were in their mid-60s after they found her lying abandoned in the snow outside a train station.

"Nobody wants them because they are afraid of trouble," says the wife.

Authorities in the town at the edge of the Gobi Desert where the couple lives now want to take the children away because they say they are too old to care for them.

"They'll have to kill me first before I'll let them take the kids away," the husband says.

I read the story, then study the photographs of the family. The father has deep creases in his face and somber eyes. His wife sits in the background of another photograph, cradling a cherubic toddler. I put the paper down and worry about the possibility that our China boycott could add even the slightest hardship to the family's lives. Rationally, I am on solid ground. The boycott isn't anything personal against China, after all, and I can't see how my family's puny buying habits could have even the tiniest impact on China's huge export economy, which in any case doesn't seem to benefit an old man forced to scavenge for a living. But the story provokes a festering concern that I am being a little mean, no matter what I tell myself.

I don't begin to feel *really* mean until a few days later, when I have an unnerving philosophical discussion with Wes over cheese sandwiches. The children and I are sitting on the front steps of my mother's house when Wes abruptly lowers his sandwich and begins to speak with a mouthful of cheese.

"Our country doesn't have a lot of food, Mama," he says.

I am surprised by his choice of topic, and his conclusion, and try to gently correct him.

"This country has a lot of food. More than any other country, in fact," I tell him.

He shakes his head.

"I don't think it does," he replies.

"No, really, it does," I insist. "Some countries don't have enough food, and lots of people in those places are hungry all the time, but here we have lots to eat. Some countries maybe you only eat a little bread or a little soup, or sometimes maybe nothing at all."

Wes pauses to consider this, then pushes for specifics.

"Like what countries?" he wants to know.

"Well, lots of places," I begin. "Many places in Africa, and some places in Asia, even some big countries like China."

Wes jumps in with a mortifying opinion.

"I'm glad they don't have enough food in China," he says.

"Why do you say that?" I ask him.

He finishes his bite of sandwich before answering.

"Because in China they are mean to their customers," he says.

"Is that why you think we are not buying things from China?" I ask. "Bad customer service?"

He nods.

My mind reels. I thought we had cleared this up weeks ago during our discussion of plastic light swords, but now Wes is drawing lines between our boycott and alleged lapses in Chinese customer service. And where did he learn the word "customer" anyway? I can say, with near certain conviction, that we have never sat around the dinner table and discussed customers or customer service. George Bush, George Foreman, hot weather, good movies, rodent problems, even our tax return— these we have discussed at the dinner table, but not customer service.

"It's not true that people are mean in China," I tell Wes now.

"Then why don't we buy China things?" he asks.

My explanation is clunky as ever.

"We are trying to buy things from other countries because China makes so many things and the factories in other countries need to sell things, too," I say.

He squints at me with one eye closed.

"That's why nobody buys things from China?" he asks.

I consider telling him that almost nobody *doesn't* buy things from China, but I am not sure I should complicate matters by trying to clear up this point. I am rescued from my indecision by the ringing of my mother's Chinese phone, which Wes rushes inside to answer.

■ ■ ■

It's my first trip to the new downtown ballpark and I should be paying attention to what's around me. The new stadium is the biggest thing to hit my hometown of San Diego in years. Larry Welk, grandson of the late music man Lawrence Welk, jogs onto the field to throw out the first pitch. I study him on the ballpark's big screen. He's chubby, deeply tanned, and wearing a T-shirt, a garment that I doubt his grandfather owned. I think I spy something familiar in the profile.

I'd like to take in the scene properly, with misty eyes and a heart swelling with memories of ball games past, but I'm distracted by the letters stamped on the outside of the package resting in my lap. It's a vinyl zip-up cooler paid for by the Welk family to promote a resort they own north of the city. The font of the letters is at least an inch high, so I can't miss the message on the package: *Made in China.*

"Do you think I should give this back?" I ask Kevin. We've settled into our seats and already he's opened his own free cooler, inspected it to his satisfaction, and tucked it under his seat.

"Keep it," he says. "I'm keeping mine."

"But look at the letters," I say.

I try to show him the *Made in China* label, but he waves me off. He's busy heckling Cincinnati and drinking a beer.

My younger brother, sitting on my other side, tries to be helpful.

"I think you should keep it because it's a gift," he says. "I bought the tickets, so they were a gift, and the cooler came with the tickets, so it's a gift, too. I think you can keep it in good conscience."

My brother's a sweet kid, but I am not so sure this cooler is a gift. It's not even wrapped. And I could have refused it at the gate, where a spirited Latina teenager shoved it into my hands as I pushed through the turnstile.

"Merry Christmas," she said.

She tossed one to Kevin behind me.

"Happy Birthday," she told him.

Now, as I study the package in my lap, I picture myself marching back to the entrance gate and handing my free cooler back to the girl. I'd work my facial features into some appropriately pathetic configuration before handing her the unopened cooler and saying something like, "I'm sorry. I cannot accept this free Chinese cooler from the Welk family. It has to do with a New Year's resolution, which I'm starting to regret, right about now. Thanks, anyway."

I cut my vision short before I have to watch what happens next. It's too excruciating to imagine what that girl might say if I tried to return the cooler, but I bet she'd have some choice words, and no shortage of them either. She isn't one to suffer fools gladly, I could see that in an instant. No, there is no way I can return my Chinese cooler if it involves facing up to that girl.

Next I entertain the option of "forgetting" the cooler under my seat after the game is over, or stuffing it into the bushes on the way out, for somebody else to find, but these strike me as unsatisfactory, and, of course, there's still the matter of Kevin's Chinese cooler. Not in a thousand years will he give it up.

Besides, I like my Chinese cooler. Correction: I love my Chinese cooler. On the outside is a detailed color illustration of the San Diego harbor, including the new ballpark and the looming towers of condos and office buildings that surround it. It's quite well done, if also spectacularly tacky. We could fill this thing with beer and chips and have grand times at the beach, starting tomorrow.

All the same, the thought of keeping the cooler makes me uneasy.

I've bent the boycott rules before—for heaven's sake, we've openly broken them on at least three or four occasions—but I feel that at a certain point you have to get serious and start toeing the line if you are going to bother to have a boycott in the first place. In my mind I do a fast rundown of our violations to date: the mandarin oranges, Kevin's ill-gotten birthday pool, the fish stickers, the paintbrushes, not to mention all the loot that entered the house on the boycott's gift technicality. Now there is the matter of the Chinese cooler, which doesn't fit neatly in the category of a gift, no matter what my younger brother says.

I turn to look at Kevin. He's stepped up his abuse of Cincinnati and started to draw looks from the people sitting around us, *appreciative* looks that egg him on.

"Cheater!" he yells after Cincinnati gets a clean single.

We are seated in the top row of the stadium so Kevin really has to put his heart into it if there's any hope of Cincinnati feeling the sting of his words. He does put his heart into it. He also tackles a basket of nachos, cons my brother into buying him a second beer, and makes friends with the bewildered French high-school exchange student sitting next to him. In other words, he has the time of his life while I clutch my Chinese cooler with moist hands and stir myself up with worry about the boycott. I don't keep track of the game's score. I'm not looking when everybody starts to do the wave and I miss my cue, standing up too late. My nachos give me a stomachache.

I'd like to be able to say that this is an unusual set of circumstances, but that's hardly the case. Variations on this scene have played out a thousand times over the years of our marriage: Kevin winning over a crowd of strangers with loud irony, and me ducking down in my seat and hoping they won't notice me.

During a quiet spell, I straighten up and turn to look behind me over the edge of the stadium. Beyond the ballpark is an industrial neighborhood of warehouses and train tracks, and beyond that I can see the deep blue of San Diego bay. Above the crowd I hear the clang of a crossing signal as a slow train rolls along the tracks. I don't know where it's headed, or what's in its cars, but that doesn't stop me from reaching a fast conclusion about what it's carrying. More stuff from China.

I turn and give Kevin another look. He's happy now, but tomorrow morning, when the crowd and the nachos are distant memories, his bitter mantra of recent days will start again. He'll zing me for three vacation crimes connected to the boycott. No squirt guns. No sunglasses for Wes. And no flip-flops on his own feet. I've been stalling on all three fronts, mostly by ignoring him, but that strategy is looking less effective by the day.

I'm running out of options. Kevin is running out of patience.

EIGHT

Red Tide

"I thought Kevin would like these," my mother says. She dangles a pair of ancient flip-flop sandals before me. "Isn't he in the market for sandals?"

They are not really a pair. They are two different sizes, one dark blue, the other faded orange with a picture of a windsurfer printed on the insole. She found them while she was cleaning out the garage. I have no idea if they were made in China. The labels probably wore off during the Carter administration. As I examine the orange one I wonder who in my family had such bad taste in beach shoes. I hope it wasn't me.

My mother is up-to-date on Kevin's footwear situation because he has been confiding in her about boycott-related hardships, including the injustice of his having to wear running shoes to the beach, "like some jerk," as he puts it. In the evenings, they murmur over drinks after dinner, and then clam up at my approach. As usual, I suspect my mother takes Kevin's side, but now, as she tries to entice me with the flip-flops, I see that this time she is playing the part of peacemaker.

"They look like something he would wear," she says.

They also look like something she would give him. Kevin grins when she tosses them at his feet later while he is standing barefoot in her kitchen. He slips his feet into them and announces his satisfaction.

"These are good-looking shoes," he says. "One of them is even my size."

I should be grateful for my mother's intercession on behalf of the boycott, but I can't help but cringe. The flip-flops are ugly shoes. Ugly, mismatched rubber sandals produced in an era of rampant bad taste, when people thought shoulder pads, feathered hair, and windsurfers on beach shoes were good ideas. I am certain from the moment Kevin tries them on that he won't confine their use to trips to the beach. I know Kevin well enough to know that he will view the mismatched flip-flops as ideal shoes for every occasion.

I'm right, of course. Over the following days Kevin rarely leaves my mother's property without the flip-flops on his feet. He wears them to the drugstore, the grocery store, the zoo, the park, the shopping mall, and, of course, the beach. He wears them everywhere we go in San Diego, and everywhere we go he draws funny looks and no shortage of comments from bemused strangers. He eats up the attention.

"It's a trend," he says after a young man in the liquor store taps him on the arm and asks him whether he realizes that his shoes don't match. "It would be a good look for you, too."

He explains to a middle-aged woman at the zoo that he couldn't buy matching flip-flops because we are boycotting Chinese products for the year and he had no other alternative.

"It was my wife's idea," he tells her. "I doubt she knew it would come to this."

I am half convinced the reason Kevin likes the flip-flops so much is because I like them so little. In fact, I loathe them. They are an affront to me on several levels, but my biggest beef is that I can no longer stroll proudly down the street with Kevin at my side. I've lost the best accessory I ever had at the end of my arm: a handsome, gregarious man with a twinkle in his eye. I'm not saying Kevin is no longer handsome, or twinkling, or walking in close proximity to me, but why marry a good-looking man with a brow like Steve McQueen if he is going to ruin the effect by wearing mismatched orange and blue flip-flops? Probably no one can focus on his aquiline nose or square jaw, either. They are too busy looking at his feet and wondering if he has lost his mind. I hurry ahead of him at the store and on the boardwalk on the beach, trying to put a healthy distance between his flip-flops and myself and hoping he won't realize what I'm up to.

"Can't you wear *regular* shoes?" I sputter one evening as we head out the door to a party.

I can tell he's been waiting for my objection.

"Matching shoes are for people with limited imaginations," he declares.

"Are you doing this just to torment me?" I ask. "For revenge? Are you and my mother colluding to humiliate me with those shoes?"

Kevin adopts a maddeningly reasonable tone.

"Not in the least," he smiles with false kindness. "What you don't seem to understand is that it's summer, and this year these are my summer shoes."

He doesn't add, *Because your boycott has locked me out of the first-run market for matching Chinese sandals.* That goes without saying.

■ ■ ■

For a week I simmer over the flip-flops and racewalk ahead of Kevin in public. Then my view of the despised sandals starts to soften. I hadn't spotted it at first, but Kevin has undergone a transformation in the days since he donned the flip-flops. I haven't heard a word of complaint from him about the boycott in days. I was so bogged down by Kevin's degraded feet that I hadn't noticed his improved attitude. I suspect there's more than mere surface cheerfulness here, too. For the first time all year, Kevin seems to be enjoying the boycott, possibly because he's found a way to use it to torture me. I force myself to be broad-minded about the matter. At least I try to be broad-minded. If I have to suffer a few indignities to win him over to my side, so be it, or so I tell myself every time I catch a good look at those shoes.

■ ■ ■

Kevin's embrace of the boycott takes many forms. At a regional food store run by aging hippies he puts a clerk to work investigating whether the pine nuts they sell are grown in China.

"I'll call you tomorrow to check in on what you find," he tells the clerk.

When he calls the next day the clerk isn't sure, so Kevin rings the company's corporate office in Los Angeles, where he gets a quick lesson in food labels. If food is grown domestically, it doesn't need a country-of-origin label, the man in corporate informs him. Kevin returns to the store and buys three packages of American-grown pine nuts.

He encourages the children to get into the swing of things. After a trip to the drugstore to look for squirt guns and water balloons, he nudges the baby in my direction and instructs her to tell me what they discovered on the shelves.

"Balloons," Sofie says with a growing frown. "China."

"No luck on the squirt guns, either," Kevin tells me cheerfully. I listen for a trace of irony in his voice. I can't hear it. "We'll keep looking."

He gets lucky in the hunt for sunglasses for Wes. He strolls into a beachside market one day and picks up the first pair he sees. *Made in Taiwan,* the label says.

That particular victory is short-lived—Sofie twists the arms off Wes's new glasses a couple of days later—but Kevin shrugs it off.

"He didn't really like to wear them anyway," he says. "No big deal."

■ ■ ■

Today Sofie does something that no toddler in America, perhaps no toddler in the world, has ever done. She is trailing after me in the toy aisle at the market when she picks up a box, peers at the underside, mutters "China" as if reading, and then returns the box to its place on the shelf. I should have seen this coming—monkey see, monkey do, after all—but I'm blindsided by her performance. My first thought is: What have I done? My next one is: Can it be undone? What sort of mother teaches her toddler to fear Chinese toys? And if she's fearful of Chinese toys, what's next? Fear of Chinese people?

I've already got my hands full with Wes, who believes bad customer service merits starvation among the Chinese masses, and now this, Lord help me, a 25-pound xenophobe, all my fault, I realize. And if this isn't enough, I've got another, more immediate concern on my hands. On my way out the door I unwisely promised the children I would bring home a toy from the grocery store, a reckless offer and more or less unforgivable at this point, given what I have learned about the origins of grocery-store toys. I take Sofie's hand and lead her to the doll section, my chest tight with foreboding.

It's there that I learn something unexpected about Barbie. She isn't entirely Chinese. She's part Indonesian. I've always been fascinated by Barbie, and not just because my parents tried with little success to ban her from my girlhood on progressive-parenting grounds. I loved her because no other doll had such great accessories. The tiny high heels. The swimsuits. The purses. All of it offensive to my parents, which made it irresistible to me. So it goes without saying that I've checked out a lot of Barbies this year, and what I've found is that Barbie invariably comes from China. Ditto for Ken, the high heels, the beach dune buggy, and the other accessories.

Yet here, surrounded by dozens of Chinese Barbies, I find a lone Indonesian doll wearing a tutu and pink tights. I am perplexed by this doll's very existence. How could it possibly be worth Mattel's while to make Barbie in Indonesia when its factories turn her out by the million in China? I consider something else. What would my mother say if I brought the doll home for Sofie to play with? Maybe she wouldn't say anything at all, which would mean I'd really hit a nerve.

It's tempting to buy the Indonesian Barbie because she only costs $6 and because it would be an entertaining way to smite my mother for giving Kevin those flip-flops, but I can't quite bring myself to do it. It's not because the flip-flops had a silver lining in the form of Kevin's improved mood, making it easier to forgive my mother. Nor am I encumbered by some lofty ideal over appropriate toys for girls; I don't think dolls make good role models, be they skinny or fat. It's not even that Sofie is too young for Barbie, although that's certainly true. I don't buy the Indonesian Barbie for the simple reason that I like the other Barbies, the Chinese ones with suntans and beach towels, better.

My restraint is rewarded further down the aisle when I locate a Mexican "popping" push toy for $5 and a bottle of American-made soap bubbles. By the time I get home I have just one remaining worry: shoring up a feeling of brotherly love in our China-bashing toddler. Uphill work, no doubt about it.

■ ■ ■

On the occasion of our 17th wedding anniversary we discover the bounty of the seashore at sunset and the allure of other people's Chinese trash.

We are on the beach in San Diego, following the children along the damp sand in the fading light, when Wes rushes back to us with a clear plastic pail in his hands. It has a magnifying glass attached to it to examine captured sea creatures.

"Can I have this?" he asks. "Is this from China?"

I ask him where he got it and he points to the soft contours of an abandoned sand castle. I look at Kevin, who lifts his shoulders and spreads his hands. I scan the beach for potential owners of the pail, but the sand is nearly empty by this hour. Its owners have abandoned the pail. That means that this Chinese pail—I take a quick look at the bottom—is Chinese trash, and Chinese trash, like Chinese gifts and Chinese hand-me-downs, is a boycott exemption.

"You can have the pail," I tell Wes.

"What about that stuff?" he asks. He turns and points up the beach, which is littered with forgotten toys, many of them near the water, where waves from the advancing tide send them tumbling across the sand. If we don't clear the place of this stuff it will end up in the gullet of some seabird or maybe a whale.

"Grab whatever you want," I say.

Half an hour later, we exit the beach parking lot with the trunk of the car loaded with Chinese shovels, pails, trowels, and buckets. As we pull into traffic I assess the boycott's impact on our vacation. True, we never found non-Chinese squirt guns or water balloons, and the kids didn't get their hands onto beach toys until our final days of vacation, but in the end we've done all right. Better than all right. Tonight we helped clear the beach of debris, something that wouldn't have occurred to us if we'd acquired beach toys through the traditional route, by buying them. I learned to get over the fact that strangers were staring at Kevin's feet—almost, anyway. The China boycott didn't rob us of surf, sand, and sunshine. Sure, we ended up with two forbidden Chinese coolers as souvenirs, but it could have been worse.

At the same time, I see trouble ahead. In a few days our vacation will be over and I will be back at home, with no working printer at my disposal, not to mention no staples. Before we left on vacation I quit my job at the business magazine to work full-time as a freelance writer, which means I can't print pages at the office anymore. In theory, I could ask Kevin to resume printing things for me at his office at the university, but I suspect that his support for the boycott is paper thin, despite his recent good cheer. The bottom line is that my printing options are running out. Indeed, they have run out. I have come to the end of my rope, printer-wise, an issue that poses a not-insignificant challenge in my chosen line of work.

I'm gazing out the window into the dark rush of traffic and feeling sorry for myself when I remember my secret weapon in the battle against Chinese printer cartridges. I can't believe my secret weapon had slipped my mind. I discovered this ace in the hole shortly before we left on vacation. It's what has allowed me to procrastinate during our holiday without too much worry; every time I got a little panicky, I'd think of this backup plan and congratulate myself for being so clever.

I resolve to deploy my secret weapon on the day that always seems to come too soon: tomorrow.

■ ■ ■

"Can't do it," the young man tells me. "Any other cartridge, but not that type."

He says something about the shape of my cartridge, or maybe the type of chemicals inside it, but I miss the details because I'm stunned by the bad news he's just delivered. He is telling me that he can't refill the empty printer cartridge that I stuck in my suitcase and hauled to California in the hope that I could refill it with toner and avoid the hunt for a non-Chinese replacement.

That cartridge was my secret weapon in the Chinese cartridge challenge. It seemed like a miracle when I learned that the nation is dotted with retail establishments whose sole purpose is refilling printer cartridges so they can be used again. I couldn't believe my good luck when a friend tossed a list of chain stores on my desk at work. When I looked up this place in my mother's phone book last night it seemed my luck was getting better still. It is just a few miles away from her house in an aging mall where I've been coming since I was a kid.

Now the walls are falling in.

"Do you think some other store could refill it for me?" I ask the young man.

He shakes his head.

"Not that type," he says. "Not refillable. Not here. Not anywhere."

I turn to leave, then think of one more thing. I ask him where the ink his company uses to refill the cartridges is made, just out of curiosity. He smiles.

"Canada," he says.

I drag my old cartridge and myself back to the car. It's miserably hot this morning. I got to the mall too early, while most of the shops were still closed. I killed an hour looking through the caged store windows at the merchandise and wondering how much of it was Chinese. I bought candy from a machine and tried to block out the sound of mall Muzak mixing with jarring strains of rap and rock blaring from inside the stores, where workers were getting ready for the day. Now this bitter pill. It's deflating to get so close to a non-Chinese printing remedy—to Canadian ink, no less—and have to turn away empty-handed.

I point the car in the direction of my mother's house and decide to spend the rest of the day doing what I've done about my printing problem for the better part of two months. Absolutely nothing.

■ ■ ■

Our house sitter must have spoiled the dog while we were on vacation in California. It's been three weeks since we've seen him but Rick looks disappointed when we tumble through the front door on a muggy August evening. He has barely worked up any momentum with his tail before he flops back onto the kitchen floor with a sigh, bored with us already.

The house is slightly more Chinese than when we left it. Also slightly improved. The house sitter replaced our mildew-streaked shower curtain with a new one made in China. The teenager we hired to cut the grass bought us a new Chinese extension cord after he mowed over the old one and chopped it in two. It isn't until a few days later that we discover something else about the house: the mice are back. This time we don't discuss a humane Chinese trap. Kevin deploys American traps and bags two of them in the first week home.

It feels like the end of our mouse problems, but later I realize it's just the beginning of the end. The end comes weeks later when we meet a mouse that refuses to take the bait. Actually, the problem is that it does take the bait—cheese and peanut butter—and still manages to escape unscathed into the abyss below the kitchen sink. I wonder if this mouse has rare talent and will elude us indefinitely, but Kevin concludes it is only a matter of time before we hear the familiar snap in the middle of the night.

"Rats are smart," he says. "Mice are stupid."

Also, as my mother and I concur, cute. I am reminded of this on the afternoon when I achieve what I wrongly concluded was impossible: the capture of a live mouse with a homemade humane trap—a homemade, humane mousetrap of my own design. Nobody I know has come close to anything like this. Our mouse-infested friends and neighbors resort to poison, cruel sticky traps that prolong mouse suffering for hours or maybe days, and traditional mousetraps that take care of business in one fast snap of wire. Nobody we know has ever attempted what I achieve in my trap.

Maybe the word *trap* is a stretch to describe what I cobble together to catch my prey; contraption is probably more like it, but the end result, a real, live mouse, caught by me, with no input from China or anybody else, is what counts.

This is how I do it. I am again at the kitchen table, looking through the day's mail, when again I hear a soft scratching noise in the cupboard below the kitchen sink. It's eerily familiar, and I find myself repeating the same strategy of previous occasions, with no real expectation of success. I rise, grab a dish towel, and tiptoe toward the cupboard. But this time, after I ease open the cupboard door and slowly pull the trash can toward me to look over the edge, I find something looking back at me: a plump brown mouse, twitching its nose and looking out of sorts at the bottom of the empty trash can. Somehow it managed to climb inside the trash can, but now it is stuck at the bottom, unable to scale the slick cliffs of plastic surrounding it.

"Don't move," I whisper to the mouse.

It doesn't.

Suddenly, I am aware that the dish towel I have gripped in my fist is of no use whatsoever. I toss it onto the counter, flash my eyes about the kitchen, and then reach for a large plastic cutting board at the end of the counter. Next, I carefully pull the trash can the rest of the way out of the cupboard and then quickly place the cutting board over the top. I can feel the plunking of the mouse as it takes a few high-flying jumps toward the top, but this mouse is not going anywhere—at least not yet.

When the kids get home they take turns peeking inside the trash can and dropping bits of old cinnamon toast on our quarry. Wes suggests the mouse would make a good pet but Kevin beats me to the obvious rejoinder.

"No way, kid," he says.

The release element of my catch-and-release plan takes place after dinner. We load the kids into the car and drive to the part of the lake where the rich people live. I ride with the trash can on my lap. It's quite uncomfortable and I can't see around the can, but I'm afraid the cutting board will slip off if I don't hold it in place. I don't want to risk the mouse clearing the rim and escaping into the car. There is only about a block left when Wes asks the question that has been in my mind since we backed out of the driveway.

"What will happen if the mouse gets free in our car?"

"Nothing will happen," I assure him, although that's not true. I've got an exit strategy. If this mouse gets loose in the Toyota I plan to fling open the door and hurl myself out onto the street, leaving every man, boy, girl, and mouse to fend for themselves. It can't hurt that much; we're only going about 12 miles per hour, and I'd have the trash can gripped against my body to cushion my fall.

We arrive at the lake without incident, pull onto a muddy embankment, and climb out of the car. I look around to see if anybody is watching, half hoping for some stranger to object, just to hear what Kevin would have to say to them. But there's nobody here but us.

Kevin lines up the children side by side and I place the trash can in front of them.

"Watch closely," I instruct the children. "This will be over quickly."

It is. I yank off the cutting board and tip the trash can on its side. The mouse makes a fast break. We watch it bound off into the weeds near the water. The whole thing takes about three seconds. The mouse doesn't look back. It's pretty anticlimatic. Wes's eyes are locked on the mouse during its brief appearance, but Sofie is looking off toward some ducks and misses the whole thing.

The release ceremony is a dud, but as we drive home I'm flying high all the same. I beat China in the humane mousetrap game, at least this once. Today, I outwitted the system, which requires that you kill a mouse if you don't want to buy Chinese or use poison or sticky traps or just give up and live with mice. Nobody can take that away from me.

A few days later, Kevin catches what again seems like the last mouse of the year in an American trap that he'd left under the sink, just in case. I feel certain that it can't be the same mouse we released at the lake— can it?—but it takes the shine off my boycott victory, all the same.

■ ■ ■

Our neighbor runs into Kevin at the store and asks him if plastic bags for groceries are made in China. My gut feeling is no. My thinking is that they can't possibly be imported because it's got to be so cheap to produce flimsy bags domestically. I have never considered this, and I have no rule to cover it.

Her question eats at me for a day or two until I think to check some old grocery bags in the laundry room. I can't find any fine print telling me where the bags were made. To be safe, I start requesting paper bags at the grocery store, although these don't say where they were made, either. I trust my instinct: paper bags seem American.

The Weakest Link draws the line at reading the fine print on plastic bags or requesting paper ones.

"That's taking things too far," Kevin says. "I'm not doing it."

I don't dare press the point.

I buy Scooby-Doo decorations for Wes's birthday cake three months before his birthday. I'm probably being paranoid, but I'm not taking any chances that the French firm that makes the decorations will relocate to China in the coming months.

The world is changing fast. You have to be ready.

■ ■ ■

It takes six hours of calls and computer searches but I finally resolve my printer cartridge dilemma. I find a place in Phoenix that sells off-brand cartridges that seem to be made in Illinois and filled with Japanese toner.

I say *seems* because I'm not certain where they are made. The man on the phone says they are assembled in Illinois, but when I ask him if that means they are *made* in Illinois he goes quiet. I'm not trying to be difficult—never am—so I try to explain.

"I'm just wondering if the plastic parts are made someplace else, like maybe China, and then just put together in Illinois," I tell him. "The word *assembled* makes me wonder."

It's quiet on his end. Then he says: "I think they are made in Illinois."

He's just trying to get rid of me, and who can blame him?

I really hope these cartridges are not made in China because the minimum order will provide enough ink for 8,000 pages. It could take me years to use that much ink. It's not that the place in Phoenix has a policy that would prevent me from returning the cartridges if they turn out to be Chinese; it's Kevin who has a policy against returning them if they turn out to be Chinese. I wince as I imagine what he'd say if I have to tell him that I'll be spending a good deal of my work day shuttling to and from the public library to print out pages because I had to return the Chinese cartridges that would have let me print pages at home.

I charge the cartridges to my Visa, hang up, and hope for the best.

CHAPTER NINE

China Dreams

Wes brings me a pen and a piece of paper and announces that it's time for him to begin his Christmas list to Santa. Christmas is nearly four months away. Outside, the molten midday air could melt an ox. But Wes isn't taking any chances that Santa will miss what's on his mind.

It's a long list and soon I can't get it off *my* mind. Wes sticks it to the front of the fridge with a magnet so that I am reminded of his unrealized toy lust every time I reach for the milk. Every day or two he pulls it off and asks me to add something new. So far, none of it looks promising in the sense that pretty much all of it looks Chinese.

One day I pluck the paper from the fridge and do a quick rundown of the likely origins of the items on his list so far:

Fire truck? Probably China.

Sno-cone maker? Absolutely China.

Superhero backpack? China.

Superhero stuff inside backpack? China.

Lunch box? My best bet, China.

Yoyo? China.

Sky Shark? China.

Robot, a blue one, plus all the other colors, too? China.

Stuffed bear? China.

Light sword? China. I've checked, and more than once.

I am intimidated by the list from the start. Then Wes introduces a new theme: police paraphernalia.

"I need handcuffs, real ones, and also a badge and a police officer's hat, a rope and a metal hook and something to write things down," he tells me one evening. He repeats what he must view as the essential item: "And some handcuffs. Real ones."

Each request feels like a nail in my coffin, especially the handcuffs. Nobody needs to tell me where plastic handcuffs come from.

■ ■ ■

I don't like to admit it, but I catch myself thinking about the boycott two days after Hurricane Katrina blows across the Gulf Coast and just as it is becoming clear to us and everybody else that the storm is a disaster of unimaginable magnitude.

On the second morning after the storm I am at the drugstore to buy toys for children at emergency shelters in our town, 80 miles from New Orleans. Here the storm felt mostly like a very windy day. It knocked out the power early and we waited in the heat for things to get really bad, but they never did. We stayed away from the windows. The dog was jumpy. The worst of it was over in a few hours. The neighbors emerged from their houses to start cleaning up their yards. We thought we'd dodged a bullet.

The next day surreal footage began to stream across the television screen and our town began to fill up with desperate people from New Orleans.

The trip to the drugstore is my first excursion out of the house since the storm hit. I pick up Malaysian coloring books, American crayons, American women's socks, and several bottles of Mr. Bubble, whose earnest labels inform me that the bubble liquid is made in Mexico and the plastic bottle that holds it is manufactured in the USA. I also pick up some diapers and formula to donate, also made in the States.

It's when I am standing in the checkout line that I start to feel queasy about what I'm doing. More than a little queasy. Ostensibly, I'm here to do something for displaced children, but my frame of mind undermines any virtue in my actions. I am still thinking of the boycott, which suggests that I am a not a serious person, or possibly even a very nice one. I would like to think of myself as someone who would forget about product labels amid the chaos and sadness of the past few days, but the China boycott stayed with me as I strolled through the drugstore and filled my basket with items for the shelters.

As I wait in line, I wonder what it would take for me to forget about the boycott. Would I still check country-of-origin labels if somebody I know died and I needed a black dress for the funeral? Would it make a difference if the deceased was a relative, or just a friend? I cannot believe I am thinking about this, and I try to stop but find I can't resist answering the question I've posed to myself. No, I could not possibly be that shallow. I decide I would definitely give up thoughts of the boycott in the event of a personal tragedy. At least I hope I would. Surely heartbreak would trump a homespun experiment in globalization. That would happen automatically, without effort, wouldn't it? I am certain that it would—almost certain. I suppose I can't be sure. I hope I never find out.

Again I try to push this gruesome bit of self-analysis from my mind, but it is difficult to do because the line is long and slow and I've got time on my hands. I am not sure I have ever had what one could call a finest hour, but I have had better ones than this.

I may even be wrong in my generous conclusion regarding my basic human decency. When I call my mother she tells me she has purchased 600 pairs of underwear to donate to evacuees. I ask if she noticed where they were made.

"I didn't think to check," she says. "It hadn't occurred to me."

Of course she didn't think to check. *Of course* it didn't occur to her. She isn't thinking of my China boycott, whose rules don't apply to her anyway. She is thinking of desperate people who have lost everything, which is the only thing I should be focused on, too. You can be certain my mother is not the sort of person who would continue to inspect product labels if she were boycotting China and somebody she knew died and she needed a dress for the funeral.

My mother checks the labels for me, then calls me back.

"Mostly Honduras," she says. "Though I think there are some American pairs in there, too."

I feel sick about myself all over again as she tells me this because I realize I take a small amount of utterly inappropriate pleasure in learning that my mother didn't just purchase 600 pairs of Chinese underwear.

■ ■ ■

I have a dream that seems like it's about Wal-Mart but is really about the China boycott.

The reason I am sure my dream is about the boycott and not about Wal-Mart is that I'm not really worried about losing to Wal-Mart, whereas sticking to the boycott is looking iffy as ever. In my dream, I sense that I am up against a giant and poorly prepared for the fight, but in reality I don't consider myself outgunned in my battle against Wal-Mart. I take a long view of the matter. One day, Wal-Mart's dark angling for "Low Prices" will catch up with it and the company will implode, Enron-style. It may take 40 years, but, in the end, I'll have the last laugh. It will be death by a thousand cuts. Just wait and see.

Eluding Chinese merchandise for the remainder of the year is another story.

In that case, I may have bitten off more than I can chew, especially as we zoom toward Christmas, the high-water mark of the Chinese sales year. I start to fret about the boycott each morning over coffee and

I keep up the worrying until bedtime. Now the boycott is chasing me in my sleep.

In my dream, I am at Wal-Mart a few days before Christmas. I wince under the lights and try to keep clear of people barreling through the aisles with shopping carts piled high with boxes of stuff from China. The crowd is restless and agitated. People waiting in a long checkout line are breaking into boxes of holiday chocolates on a display table next to the line. They bite into the chocolates and return the half-eaten pieces to the boxes. For some reason I am looking for the store manager, Mr. Joshua, but nobody can tell me where to find him. Several aisles away, in the middle of the store, I see a conveyor belt carrying gold-colored boxes up to a second floor. I walk over, look around to see if anybody is watching, then scramble onto the conveyor belt. It carries me upstairs through a square in the tiled ceiling to a dim, oak-paneled office. A female security guard steps out of the shadows as I climb off and step onto burgundy-colored carpet.

"This is Mr. Joshua's office," the dream guard says sternly. "You are not supposed to be here."

The next thing I know she directs me back onto the conveyor belt, which has reversed itself and is now heading downstairs. I climb on and ride it down. At the bottom, two security guards wait for me. There are more people in the checkout line now, and they are edgier than ever. More shoppers are ripping into the boxes of chocolate. This seems like behavior verging toward a store riot, like the final collapse of civilized society in one fell swoop, but the security guards don't seem concerned with the illicit chocolate eaters. They focus on me, their eyes brimming with disdain. *I'm not the criminal here,* I want to shout, but when I open my mouth no sound comes out. One of the guards grips my arm and marches me toward the exit. The automatic doors glide open onto a pool of darkness. The guard shoves me forward and I stumble out into the unknown, my arms flailing to protect against unseen perils that lie ahead of me in the black air.

I open my eyes and stare into the darkness of our bedroom, wary of falling back to sleep.

As the dream suggests, I am worried, with good reason.

Take Wes's Christmas list, which is looking more and more hopeless. The other day he asked me to add a monster truck, a whistle, and a locker. As I add these items to the list I repeat one word to myself: *China, China, China.*

Holiday catalogs begin to arrive in the mailbox. Predictably, they are full of Chinese stuff, though the catalog companies don't like to admit it. I call a catalog of holiday decorations to ask about a Thanksgiving-themed tablecloth and turkey-shaped vinyl place mats that the catalog describes as "imported." The customer-service representative tells me that both are made in China, information that comes as a relief, because otherwise I might be tempted to buy them and the last thing this house needs is more junk in it, especially junk with a turkey theme.

At the craft superstore I encounter six-foot fake Chinese Christmas trees already hung with Chinese ball ornaments. Next to the trees is a larger-than-life plastic Chinese Santa Claus that would scare the dickens out of the children. I count the rows of Chinese Christmas decorations. Fifteen, double-sided, reaching 12 feet toward the ceiling.

I fortify my resolve with encouragement from unexpected sources. "Just do it," Nike tells me. "One day at a time," a bumper sticker advises. *Carpe diem,* I tell myself, and try not to get bogged down with thoughts of the holidays.

It's difficult not to get bogged down because everything tells me Christmas is coming. Sofie begins her own list to Santa. It has five items on it: blue robot fighter, Thomas the Train hideaway, play kitchen, a blue dog, and a baby stroller. Her list is as Chinese as her brother's.

Even my mother won't let me forget about what lies ahead.

"Have you started your Christmas shopping yet?" she asks one night. "I'm almost finished."

"I've started worrying but that's as far as I've taken it," I say. I add, "I work best under pressure," although that is not true.

A young woman from the cable company calls to say they can install cable service for $2, then allow us to have four months of service at half price. Her offer sounds too good to be true, which turns out to be the case. When the cable guy arrives, he says it will be $75 for the installation and wonders why in the world I think they should give us four months of discount service? His bad news turns out to be for the best. During our confused exchange in the living room I take a fast look at the lasso of cable that hangs at his hip. *Made in China,* it says. The upshot of the encounter is that we don't get cable and I also realize that I don't have a boycott rule to deal with home repairmen and others who ply their trade with Chinese tools.

The boycott grabs the attention of one of the ladies at the children's preschool. She tells me she has started to check the tags on Sofie's shoes and clothes to make sure they aren't from China. She makes it clear that she doesn't think a year without China is possible, or sensible.

"Ya'll are going to slip up," she says. "And when you do, ya'll are going to hear about it from me."

"It won't happen," I tell her. "By the way, made in China hand-me-downs from her cousin are not against the rules."

"Fair enough," she says.

Sofie increasingly resembles an English sheepdog, unable to see through the curtain of hair that covers her face.

"Her hair grows forward," our hair stylist explains after a haircut, which doesn't help much. "What she needs is barrettes."

Barrettes come from China

Sofie has the good sense to help herself. After we get home from a party I discover a barrette clutched in her hand. She must have found it on the floor of our friends' house. I don't know which little girl might have lost it, and sheepishly I neglect to call to find out. For the next few days I blissfully clip Sofie's hair into a fountain on the top of her head. She can see clearly for the first time in weeks.

We lose the barrette in a matter of days. Sofie's face vanishes again behind a fringe of blond hair.

■ ■ ■

About a week after my Wal-Mart dream I have another dream about the boycott. This time, I dream that big-wave surfer Laird Hamilton is giving me windsurfing lessons in the cobalt waters off Hawaii. A reasonable person might suggest that this dream also has nothing to do with the boycott. The Weakest Link is among those to miss the connection.

As with the Wal-Mart dream, I know better.

"Windsurfing with Laird Hamilton, eh?" Kevin remarks over his coffee the next morning. "I'd say that's progress over your dream about Donald Rumsfeld for sure."

I take a deep breath so I have enough air to set Kevin straight.

"Don't you see? My dream wasn't about windsurfing with Laird Hamilton, it was about facing impossible odds," I say. "Laird Hamilton conquers 40-foot waves that should kill people. Waves as big as buildings. Waves that can snap his neck or pulverize him on the shards of coral beneath the water if he makes one wrong move. That's the point. He does the impossible. He slays giants and lives to tell about it. And I'm supposed to slay a giant, too, by making it through the holidays without buying anything from China."

Kevin looks doubtful.

"Maybe you just have a crush on Laird Hamilton," he suggests. "You can admit it. Doesn't bother me."

I shake my head.

"All women have crushes on Laird Hamilton," I say. "That's a given. This dream was something else. This dream was a *message*."

Kevin pulls down the ends of his mouth to signal his disbelief in cosmic messages and his understanding that, until this morning, I didn't believe in them either.

"Anything you say," he says.

I ignore his skepticism. What the Weakest Link doesn't realize is that things are suddenly looking up, vis-à-vis the boycott. I'm starting to see specks of blue sky through the veil of gloom that had shrouded my view of the holiday season ahead of us. The Laird Hamilton dream makes me sit up and take notice of a series of small victories that I might have missed otherwise, starting with the day Kevin brings home a bag of Portuguese corks so that he and the kids can make homemade bottle rockets with vinegar and baking soda. They blast the corks 30 feet into the air, producing high-impact fun typically available only through Chinese fireworks.

The Portuguese corks are just the beginning. I stop squinting and dig out Kevin's glacier glasses. I make up my mind to maintain my dignity when I'm at a red light and people stare at me. I pretend I don't notice their gaze and keep my eyes on the light.

The off-brand printer cartridges arrive. The outside of the cardboard box says *Made in USA* but I worry that maybe it's only the box that is made domestically. I ought to call the company again to sort this out once and for all, but somehow I don't get around to it. Instead, I do what Laird Hamilton must do when he points his surfboard down the face of a monster wave that could be the death of him: I *think positive*. I decide that I will believe what the cardboard box tells me: that its contents were made in the USA. I will trust the man at the Phoenix warehouse who told me the cartridges were made in Illinois, not just assembled there. I will trust my good fortune and never look back. I will *believe*, and on days when I can't manage that, at least I will embrace a state of denial about the shadow of the monster wave at my back.

After dismissing my dressmaking skills in the past, Sofie unexpectedly requests that I make her a tutu. I buy Mexican ribbon and American tulle at the craft superstore and have it ready to go in 10 minutes. I watch her twirl off across the room, her tutu tied on over blue jeans.

Even catalogs full of Chinese merchandise don't scare me the way they did just a week ago. I catch Wes flipping through the pages of a catalog of hundreds of children's Halloween costumes, most of them imported, which to me means made in China. He pauses at a page advertising a 10-piece policeman's outfit that comes with a ticket book, handcuffs, a whistle, and other law enforcement accessories. I beat Wes to the punch before he has time to start begging me for it.

"This year Halloween will be special," I tell him. "This year I am going to sew your costume. I think you would look handsome in something involving a cape. Like a vampire. Or maybe a prince."

Wes looks at me and opens his mouth, but I turn and hurry from the room before he can object.

Speaking of objections, I've even come up with a strategy to guard against potential future allegations by Wes that Christmas is a dud as a result of the boycott, a distinct possibility given the abundance of Chinese items on his list to Santa. My strategy is desperate, that I admit, but I suspect it will work. I promise Wes that he and Sofie can select three toys of their choice on the first day of the new year, when the China boycott is officially over.

"Three things. Whatever you want," I say. "I promise I won't even look at the labels to check where anything is from."

"Three things?" he asks.

"Three things."

He wants to pin me down on this.

"Any three things?" he asks.

I start to lose my nerve.

"Nothing too expensive," I say.

"Chinese things?" he wants to know.

"Chinese things, Mexican things, Egyptian things, any kind of things," I assure him. "Three of them."

There's even bad news about Wal-Mart, which is good news to me. I read that it's being sued for alleged labor abuses in the factories of its overseas suppliers. Like I said before, when it comes to Wal-Mart's demise, it will be death by a thousand cuts. Only a matter of time.

■ ■ ■

On a Friday night in mid-September we hire a babysitter to watch the kids. We don't head out the door for dinner and a movie. We head upstairs, to the attic, to repair the roof.

We heard a mysterious bang against the house during the hurricane but we didn't learn until today what caused it. It turns out the storm blew off a metal cap that runs along the top of the house, leaving a three-inch gap about 15 feet long at the highest point of the roof. It's been mostly dry in the days since the storm, so we didn't realize there was a problem until today, during a downpour, when I walked into Wes's bedroom to discover water leaking through his ceiling lamp onto the floor. We called a few roofers but they were busy with weightier projects, so it falls to us to patch the damage until they can get here in a week.

There is a knot of anxiety in my stomach as I follow Kevin up a ladder in Sofie's closet and into the attic, a dark, dank no-man's-land of electrical wiring and rotten pink insulation. We have to crawl on our hands and knees because the space is so tight. My hands brush against the wires that crisscross the insulation. I worry that I will be electrocuted. I try not to think about rats.

At one point, I have to squeeze after Kevin through a narrow hole in a piece of plywood to reach the part of the roof where the gap is. For a moment, I am not sure I can do it, but I don't want to risk the chance that Kevin will electrocute himself up here, alone in the heat and darkness. So I force myself through the hole and try not to touch anything that might kill or bite me.

The other day I convinced myself that I would not continue to think about the boycott in the event of a death in the family, but during our trip to the attic I realize this may not be the case. My debut in roof repair involves cutting pieces of plastic sheeting from a large roll and positioning the pieces over the gap in the roof while Kevin staple-guns them into place. During a break, while Kevin is maneuvering around, cursing and questioning the effectiveness of our technique in keeping the rain out, I point my flashlight on the bag the sheeting came in. I turn the light until the yellow beam finds what I'm looking for. "Another quality product by Warp Bros., Chicago, Ill.," it says on the package. There is an American flag with the words *Made in USA* next to it. My heart sprouts wings and takes flight.

So who am I kidding? If I am still thinking about the boycott while risking electrocution and rat attack in a filthy attic in 100-degree heat, then it is probably reasonable to conclude that there isn't any circumstance in which I would lose sight of it.

■ ■ ■

"Piano lessons," I tell Kevin. "Same as last year."

Kevin wants to know what I want for Christmas, which is alarming, because he is an easygoing fellow who doesn't normally start thinking about Christmas until December 10, at the earliest. If he is thinking about Christmas in September then things must be looking desperate.

"But you never signed up for the lessons," he says. "So I didn't really get you anything last year."

"I know, but still they were such a good Christmas gift," I assure him. "They didn't cost us a thing, and it convinced several of my friends that you have the soul of a poet. They thought it was romantic. I think you may have gotten some of the other husbands in trouble because they couldn't come up with anything nearly that good."

"You have friends who think it's romantic that I didn't get you anything for Christmas?" he asks.

"They don't know the lessons never happened," I say. "What they know is that you came up with the idea of piano lessons, all by yourself, which is groundbreaking territory for husbands and Christmas presents, as far as I know."

He sighs.

"All right," he says. "But this time I am going to find you a teacher and sign you up so you actually take the lessons."

I smile.

"Suit yourself," I say.

I am pleased with myself. Again I have ducked the boycott's restrictions and saved us a bundle in the process, since there's not a chance that Kevin or I will get around to tracking down a piano teacher. Well done, I tell myself.

■ ■ ■

One evening, Wes strolls into the room gripping a dog-eared toy catalog. He holds open a page and points to a photograph of a remote-controlled truck called a Morphibian. The description claims it can "tackle the most rugged terrain and churn through water."

"Can I have this for Christmas?" Wes asks.

I give a politician's answer, which means I give him no answer at all.

"Put it on your list to Santa," I say. "We'll see what he thinks."

CHAPTER
TEN

Meltdown

"What are janitor pants?" I ask Kevin.

He stares at me for a long moment before stating the obvious.

"Pants like janitors wear," he says. "Flat in the front, straight legs, a place to hook your keys."

It's 6:40 in the morning and Kevin has just announced that he will wear any pants I buy him so long as they are janitor pants. I look down to study the open page of the J.Crew catalog in my lap. It doesn't mention janitors or members of any other occupation.

"Do you mean chinos?" I venture. I hold up the catalog so Kevin can inspect a photograph of cotton pants. He sighs to let me know that my questions are wearing him out, then leans forward from his spot on the sofa between the children and squints in the semidarkness at the page.

"Yeah, those are janitor pants," he says. He snorts. "Chinos. Who ever heard of those?"

He returns his attention to the glow of the television screen.

There's been a surprise development in our marriage. Kevin has proclaimed, with several witnesses present, that he is willing to wear whatever I buy him if it means I will stop making snide comments about his wardrobe, which mostly consists of frayed khakis and logo-covered T-shirts he gets for free for participating in local 10K running races. That's his standard ensemble on his teaching days, when he's comparatively fussy about his looks. Things get really casual on the weekends when he hauls out pants and shirts with holes as big as small dogs in them—sometimes bigger than small dogs.

My sister-in-law is among those in attendance when Kevin signals that he is ready to undergo a fashion overhaul if I am up to the challenge of leading it. When Kevin isn't looking, she gives me an encouraging nod from across the room. Sometimes, when we're running low on topics for conversation, we trade wistful critiques of Kevin's limited fashion sense.

"Such a waste," she'll say, shaking her head. "You really should do something about that."

She's probably right, but I have mixed feelings about a wardrobe intervention. Part of me admires Kevin's lackadaisical attitude about his appearance. Cluelessness in clothing is part of what makes Kevin Kevin. He is not vain in the least. I never catch him sneaking sidelong glances at his reflection in store windows. His battery of cosmetic aids consists of an ancient comb and a razor blade. If anybody is vain about Kevin's looks, it's me. And that's not my only hesitation about a Kevin makeover. I don't want to risk allegations of playing the role of overbearing shrew to a cowed husband or, God forbid, mother figure to him. Then again, how often does a wife get an offer to play a grown-up version of dolly dress-up with her husband, with his endorsement?

Kevin puts one condition on the deal: "Just don't make me go shopping with you," he says.

I've stalled for days, uncertain if he really means what he says, but when I wake this morning I am ready to accept my mission. It's still dark outside when I start flipping through the J.Crew catalog and holding up pages for Kevin's inspection. I get the nod on new janitor pants at approximately 6:41 A.M. Minutes later I am at the kitchen table dialing the catalog's customer-service number. I get a young man who sounds surprised but is obliging when I tell him I'd like to know the origins of the chinos and a dandy belt made of colorful ribbon that Kevin agrees would "look good with janitor pants." The young man puts me on hold. I listen to disco music for seven minutes.

"Are you still there?" the young man asks when he returns.

He reports that the pants are made in Hong Kong and the belt in China. I tell him I'd like to go ahead with the pants but I will pass on the Chinese belt. I sense him hesitate.

"May I ask why you don't want the belt?" he inquires, tentatively. "My supervisor and I were wondering why you wanted to know where these things were from. People don't usually ask about that."

I tell him I'm trying to go a whole year without buying anything made in China, to see how hard it is to do.

"It's an experiment," I say.

He laughs. "That's a cool idea."

He tells me that all the catalog's shoes are Italian and its cashmere items are from Mongolia but that he doesn't know the origin of the other items. I tell him that maybe I'll call J. Crew back in January to order the belt from China, overtly flirting by this point. I cannot resist admirers of the boycott.

"I hope I answer the phone when you call," he says.

We hang up and I wander back into the living room and throw myself onto the sofa. Then I start to think about Hong Kong, and whether it isn't actually a part of China, and whether maybe I shouldn't get back up, march back into the kitchen, and call back my new friend at J. Crew to cancel my order of two pairs of possibly Chinese janitor pants. I fret about this possibility for a few minutes, thinking of Kevin in his wardrobe of holey pants. Then I remember who can help me sort out this mess: the Central Intelligence Agency.

Months ago, when I asked my younger brother, who spent many years living in Asia, whether Hong Kong is now a part of China, he told me that he thought it was some sort of "special administrative region of China." I thanked him, though it sounded like a lot of nonsense to me. What in the world is a special administrative region? A meaningless term, in my opinion. Couldn't my brother, with his big brain and worldly insights, come up with a better explanation of Hong Kong's place in the world?

No, he could not. Apparently, the CIA couldn't either. When I visit the CIA World Factbook on the Internet to read about Hong Kong, it describes it as a "special administrative region of China." Even worse, its official name, according to the CIA, is "Hong Kong Special Administrative Region," and President Hu Jintao, China's president, is its chief of state. July 1 is a national holiday celebrated as Hong Kong Special Administrative Region Establishment Day. This is a disturbing development, not only because Hong Kong Special Administrative Region is the least poetic place name I can imagine, but also because I am quite sure I have purchased at least a couple of items from Hong Kong over the past months. I should have brushed up on Asian geopolitics months ago, when the boycott was in its infancy.

My missteps involving Hong Kong seem bad enough but then I recall that I also bought Sofie a dress from Macau, the old Portuguese region of Hong Kong. So I look up Macau in the CIA World Factbook. Its official name? Macau Special Administrative Region—of China.

So where does this leave Kevin's new janitor pants? Should I return them? Or can I keep them and simply avoid Hong Kong and Macau for the rest of the year? I pore over my choices, and then decide that the boycott is a work in progress, inevitably imperfect, like so much in life.

Kevin gets to keep his new janitor pants.

■ ■ ■

We take the kids to breakfast at a popular and breathtakingly filthy greasy spoon. The waitress brings Wes a place mat and a box of four Chinese crayons. I fool with my cutlery during the wait to keep my eyes away from the walls, which are speckled with ancient bits of egg.

On the underside of the handle of my knife it says *Made in Brazil*. I don't find anything printed on my fork or the bottom of my cup and saucer, and then the waitress brings our food and I forget about China for a while. When we get home I decide to pursue something that's been on my mind for the past few days: determining whether Hannah Wiggins is Chinese.

Hannah Wiggins is the doll on page 2 of a toy catalog that arrived in the mail this week. She comes with a set of four interchangeable wigs made of yarn that attach to her head with Velcro. "Like most girls, she likes to change her hair when she changes her clothes," the catalog says. In the photograph Hannah Wiggins is wearing bright orange-and-red striped tights. Sofie also owns orange-and-red striped tights. I was smitten. Hannah Wiggins will make a perfect Christmas present for Sofie.

The question is whether Hannah Wiggins, like almost every other doll sold in America, is from China. I settle on the sofa with the catalog, take a deep breath, and dial the number. Paul comes on the line right away. I give him the item number, and then ask for the country of origin. There's a pause of about 10 seconds, and it's so quiet that I'm not sure whether Paul is still there. While he's away I silently repeat to myself, "Please say Vietnam, please say Vietnam."

"China," Paul says. I choke back a moan.

"Thanks, that's all I needed," I say, and abruptly hang up. I am too depressed to flirt with Paul.

I pout for a couple of hours and then I do what I often do when I'm feeling blue. I call my mother. I give her a rundown of recent family news in a breezy manner, and then casually slip in the bit about the Hannah Wiggins doll. I manage to mention the names of both the catalog and the doll—twice. She sees right through me.

"Which catalog did you say?" she asks.

I tell her, then add, "I'm not suggesting you buy the doll for her, of course. I'm just telling you what happened. Just so you know what's going on around here."

I hang up and spend a few minutes feeling like a guilty liar. Soon Wes locates me on the sofa and makes a request that transforms my mood from one of guilt to trepidation. He wants me to add something else to his list to Santa.

"Vampire fangs," he says. "But they need to be really sharp ones."

Sharp, plastic, Chinese vampire fangs, I think. Ouch.

■ ■ ■

A friend of mine wants to know what our plans are for the New Year.

"Are you and China getting back together?" she asks.

She tells me that she tried recycling her old boyfriend back in college, but that they didn't stay together long after their reunion.

"Of course, we were never in as deep as you and China were," she says. "In our case, it wasn't meant to last."

I have to admit I haven't given the matter much thought. I've always considered the China boycott a trial separation, a yearlong odyssey to get a little breathing room before an inevitable reconciliation based on convenience rather than love. I read about people going off the grid and living in compounds in Idaho without electricity or running water, but the truth is I am not sure that I could give up for all eternity something as fundamental to modern life as Chinese merchandise. I can't see myself living like this for the long term. I'm not sure I can see myself living like this for next two and a half months. The first nine and a half months of the year have been interesting enough, but now a Christmas without Chinese gifts under the tree looms like a date with the executioner. I'm exhausted.

Besides, as I discover this week, there is also the matter of the China boycott's impact on a certain small boy's happiness, which sometimes rests on possession of something purple, plastic, and Chinese. It's a lesson I learn during a family trip to Target for Halloween decorations. The trip is Kevin's suggestion. I should have sensed trouble from the beginning. After all, nobody knows better than I do where the decorations for every American holiday are made. But it's a crisp fall Saturday with the feel of luck in a wide blue sky and I think maybe that lucky feeling will extend to the holiday decorations department at Target.

It does not.

It's all Chinese. Every bit of it, as I should have known. The gauzy, polyester spider webs, the fake hands with moving fingers, the electric jack-o-lanterns, and the light-up boulder with the ominous message "Go back!" on it—it is all off-limits. Wes's eyes glow with anticipation as we move through the aisles, checking the *Made in China* labels and hoping to catch a break. The gleam in his eye fades as we encounter one Chinese item after another. Twenty minutes after we enter the store, when it's clear that China owns Halloween and our shopping cart is still empty, we gather in a morose circle at the end of an aisle. That's when Wes's courage leaves him. His shoulders sag as if they've got the full weight of the world upon them. He looks at me and starts to cry.

"Can't this be a special time because it's Halloween so we can buy things from China?" he wails.

He grips my arm. His body droops. Forty pounds of miserable boy strain my wrist. My firstborn child, my curly-haired prince, is desperate for the happiness that comes from owning something new, glowing, and plastic. I notice that he doesn't look once at the Weakest Link, who stands a few feet away holding the baby and glaring at me. Wes knows instinctively that I am the source of his agony, the guarder of the boycott, the enemy of delicious and forbidden Chinese items, the force whose will he must break with piteous cries. My heart thumps fast. My wrist is hurting. Wes is killing me.

For a moment I can't think of a thing to say, but then, with a fleet cynicism worthy of a Vegas con man, I remember the words that have saved me on so many occasions over the past year.

"Next time," I say. My voice is thin and unconvincing, even to me, but I hope Wes doesn't notice. "Next Halloween we can get anything you want."

But Wes is done with waiting for next time. He has had enough of happiness deferred and Chinese trinkets denied. He's getting more desperate by the moment. He starts yanking on my arm.

"Let me show you the one thing I want," he pleads. "It's just one little thing."

I let him pull me along as my mind spins and I try to come up with a way to turn this ship around before it crashes on the rocks and sinks to the bottom. We trudge past towering stacks of blinking plastic heads and superhero costumes, all undoubtedly Chinese. Wes leads me around a corner to a table display of electric pumpkins of various sizes set out in alternating rows of orange and purple. He releases my arm and lifts a small orange pumpkin towards me. It is covered with tiny orange and black beads and wears a diabolical grin of triangular teeth.

"This is what I want," he says. "See? It's small."

Wes looks at me with puffy eyes in which a glimmer of hope still flickers. He has the orange pumpkin pressed to his chest in a death grip. Something inside me is sinking, fast.

"Can't we cut the rules this time?" he asks, his voice almost a whisper. He gestures toward the rows of larger electric pumpkins. "I don't want a big one, just this little one."

And then, in case I missed it before, he repeats, "It's small."

I stand frozen and silent while that thing sinking inside of me falls faster into the depths. Can the China boycott really have been so hard on Wes? No, I tell myself. Impossible. I would have caved back in January if I thought he was truly suffering. Of course, I realize he hasn't suffered a bit in the crushing-poverty sense of real suffering, but he also hasn't suffered in comparison to his preschool colleagues in generally overindulged, middle-class America. He may have heard the words "No," and "Next time," and "How about a Lego set?" more often than he would like, but that is not the same thing as suffering. Of that I'm also certain. Absolutely, almost certain.

Sure, he's kept his eyes on the prize of a Chinese light sword somewhere in his future, but there's been no angst in giving up other Chinese toys, at least not until now. He hasn't been restless and bored. He has sailed through his days like he always has, on a smile and a nonstop stream of jokes with punch lines understandable only to other four-year-olds. He's been easily appeased with Legos and Italian felt pens, and it isn't as if he had no new toys at all. Not long ago I found him a plastic bubble sword made in Taiwan that makes six-foot soap bubbles. The enormous bubbles float above the grass and transform our dog Rick into 80 pounds of snapping, growling, bubble-destroying, fur-flying artillery. If that isn't entertainment, I don't know what is.

And Wes has had something else at his disposal 24/7 to see him through lean times in toyland: the boundless energy of his father, a high-velocity pied piper with an entertainment value for children that falls midway between a puppy and a chimpanzee in pants. Hardly a day goes by when Kevin isn't flinging the children into the air, impersonating a gorilla or helping them build towering forts in the living room that endanger the well-being of the children themselves and the lamp next to the sofa and force me to sit on cushionless sofa springs while I watch the evening news. And I am no humorless matron on the lookout for fun-quashing opportunities. I let the children ride scooters in the house, chase each other at full-speed around the kitchen table, and stick drooly fingers in cookie dough. Once we pitched an outdoor tent in the living room. It was there for weeks. How can Chinese toys compete with that?

So, no, I tell myself, Wes hasn't suffered as a result of the boycott. Not for a moment. Out of the question. Ridiculous.

Yet when I look into the eyes that gaze back into mine as I stand in the Halloween section of Target, I cannot deny that these are suffering eyes. There is no getting around it. I am looking into big, blue, suffering eyes that plead for compassion and a little orange pumpkin. Such a small request, these suffering eyes tell me. Suddenly, my head feels hot. My mouth is dry. Maybe Wes has suffered all along, it occurs to me, and maybe I've just been in denial.

Suddenly, I am ready to throw in the towel, to ditch the boycott and chuck the orange pumpkin into our cart, maybe even throw in a fake hand and some polyester spider webs. After nine and a half months of artfully swatting away requests for light swords and monster trucks, at this moment I can't think of a single thing to say, except good-bye to the boycott and yes to my beloved son with the big blue suffering eyes. But when I open my mouth to speak I don't say yes. I say something else entirely.

"We're almost done with our China experiment," I tell Wes. "You've just got to hang on a little longer, okay?"

Then I add a bribe, as I have done so often over the months.

"We can choose a Lego toy for you right now," I say. "And next year we can get an electric pumpkin. Even a big one, if you like. Maybe two of them, an orange one and a purple one."

Wes is still slumping as I hold out my hand for the pumpkin.

And then, to my surprise, he relents. The anguish drains out of him all at once. He looks at me in silence for a moment, then nods and wipes his streaming nose with the back of his shirtsleeve. He hands over the little orange pumpkin. I put it back on the display table. Then I hold out my hand and he puts his fingers into mine.

"Let's go look at Legos," I say.

The rest of the trip through the store is routine. I pick up Korean socks for Sofie, a Danish Lego police truck for Wes, and a second one for a little boy's birthday party later in the day. I tell myself that I should feel relieved that the boycott has been rescued from another mishap, but in fact I feel dejected. My win in the battle against the electric pumpkin is a hollow victory, for several reasons. For starters, it suggests to me that the thumping in my chest couldn't be my heart because I haven't got one. Second, Kevin hasn't stopped shooting dirty looks at me since it became clear that the boycott would throw cold water on our family Halloween fun. He was looking forward to decorating the house for Halloween. We were all looking forward to decorating the house for Halloween. Now I've put the brakes on that. And I made Wes cry, even if the Lego truck has patched him up for now.

The bottom line is that nobody likes a spoilsport, especially me, especially when the spoilsport is me.

I gaze out the window of the Toyota on the way home and search for a silver lining. I tell myself that I have neatly solved the matter of Wes's discontent. I console myself with the comfortable idea that his unhappiness over the pumpkin is merely *surface* unhappiness, not the real stuff that runs to the bones and sticks with you for the long haul. I have purchased two and a half months of patience—the 70 days until the boycott's official end on December 31—on Wes's part with a $6 Lego truck and promises of electric pumpkins in the new year. And Kevin won't pout for long. It's not in his nature to play the skeleton at the feast. All of which is to say that while it wasn't fun, I have managed to spare the boycott the indignity of another purchase of illicit Chinese merchandise. By the time we pull back into our driveway I figure the case of the orange pumpkin is ancient history. Case closed.

It turns out I'm wrong about that.

That evening on the sofa, just after we finish a story and shortly before bed, Wes falls apart again, suddenly, completely, and without warning.

"Why can't we buy China things anymore?" he wails out of the blue, curling up on the sofa beside me as if in pain. "I don't want to not buy China things anymore. It's too hard."

I am caught off guard. I open my mouth to remind him of the Lego truck, but now I see with absolutely clarity that a Lego truck is an insufficient remedy to this level of agony, and that maybe I was even wrong about surface unhappiness versus the real thing. I watch Wes knock a book to the floor as he writhes with inner turmoil. I don't look at Kevin or Sofie, who huddle together at the far end of the sofa and condemn me with their eyes.

Then, out the blue, comes a small miracle. I have a vision of something I'd forgotten about for months: the metal money box in the top drawer of Wes's bedroom dresser. At last count it held $19, although I believe I may have borrowed a five and slipped in an IOU in its place when I was out of cash one evening and in a hurry to meet a friend. I turn to Wes with a peace offering.

"All right," I say. "You can buy the pumpkin, but with your own money. Mama's not buying it for you. I'll drive you back to the store in the morning and help you give the money to the cashier, but it will be you buying the pumpkin from China, not me."

Wes sits up and rubs at his eyes. He sniffs hard to try to pull himself together.

"But if I don't have enough money will you give me some?" he asks.

I tell him I think he has enough money.

"Just this one thing from China," I add. "Then we don't buy China things again until after Christmas. Not a thing."

I am not sure I have made the right decision, but Kevin affirms it.

"You're not so bad," he tells me later as we climb into bed.

He sounds relieved, as if he's been wrestling with the question of my goodness versus badness and only recently resolved the matter in my favor.

■ ■ ■

"I'm happy that we're buying China things at last," Wes tells me the following morning as the two of us settle into the Toyota. I try to catch his eye in the rearview mirror.

"You are buying a China thing, not me," I remind him. "And it's just this once."

I can feel Wes's adoring eyes on the back of my head as we pull onto the freeway. It takes us 10 minutes to get back to Target. He hums to himself the whole way. At the store, Wes abruptly shifts his attachment from a small orange pumpkin to a small purple one. The price tag says $4.99. I keep my fingers off the bills as he hands his money to the cashier. He is beside himself as she hands him the pumpkin in his own plastic bag. He floats beside me as we cross the parking lot to the car, peeking into the shopping bag several times to make sure the purple pumpkin is still in there, and still his.

At home, Wes plugs the pumpkin into a wall socket and sets it on the back of a sofa against a window so that passersby can admire it. I watch him with a mix of guilt at abusing the boycott—again—and pleasure at seeing him enjoy his little hunk of glowing plastic. He sits by the window waiting for somebody to walk by the house so he can wave and point out his pumpkin to them.

After a few minutes, he turns to study me with somber eyes.

"Mama," he begins. "Will you have two more babies and when they get here will you tell them that it's okay to buy China things because I don't want them to cry all the time and you can tell them that when they are zero but not until they are older?"

I get his drift, despite the problems with his grammar.

■ ■ ■

My mother calls to ask for Christmas gift suggestions for the kids, which is odd, because she's spent the past few weeks bragging to me about how she's almost finished with her holiday shopping.

"What's that?" she asks, when I tell her that Wes would be thrilled with anything with a Scooby-Doo theme.

"What's what?" I say.

"Scooby-Doo?"

I am confused. It sounds like my mother just asked me who Scooby-Doo is.

"You've never heard of Scooby-Doo?" I ask, incredulous.

"Never," she says. "Is that something new?"

I tell her who, or rather what, Scooby-Doo is, refraining from mentioning that he has served as canine antihero to at least a couple of generations of American children, including her own. I also don't mention that in all likelihood anything that she might find that bears Scooby-Doo's image is Chinese and that I'd rather not know about it if that's the case.

She calls back the next day to tell me that she has found a Scooby-Doo-themed air popcorn maker.

"The kernels come shooting out of his mouth," she says.

I don't ask where the machine was made. Instead, I ask my mother what she would like for Christmas.

"I'm old," she says. "I don't need anything."

"Good," I say. "Then I can cross you off the list."

This theme is an extension of one my mother took up during our visit to San Diego in the summer. When I commented then about her lack of a rack for drying dishes, resulting in a jumble of plates and utensils in the sink, she responded that she was too old to get full use out of a new one so what was the point? She'd been using a salad colander for the same purpose, although, as I made the mistake of pointing out to her, with mixed results.

"I could buy you a dish rack," I told her. "I think they cost about $5 at the grocery store."

"Don't you dare," she said.

I didn't.

This time, I don't buy her don't-buy-me-a-thing act. She wants something for Christmas, but for some reason known only to her she doesn't want to come right out and admit it. My mother can be difficult to decipher.

Certainly her grandchildren have no trouble admitting that they'd like something for Christmas. Lately, when I ask Wes if he'd like me to read him a story, he sometimes asks me to read his list to Santa to him instead. Each time I remind him that there's no guarantee that Santa will bring him any of the things on the list, but I can tell he's not listening.

"It's going to be great to have a light sword," he tells me, dreamy-eyed.

■ ■ ■

Wes's unshakeable faith in Christmas is one of several humbling developments. To begin, I have discovered something unsettling about Wes's Italian tennis shoes, which he has worn for nearly seven months. They are not Italian.

I come to this surprise conclusion in a roundabout way, after Wes's godmother asks me what size shoes he wears. Her question prompts me to take a look inside one of his shoes where, under the tongue, it says either *Made in CSR* or *Made in CSA*. The printing is worn thin so I'm not certain what it says, although clearly it does not say *Made in Italy*. Then again, it also does not say *Made in China*, so it could be worse. In any case, Wes's toes are inching perilously near to the end of his shoes, meaning I may be in the hunt for new non-Chinese tennis shoes before too long. I decide not to think about that for now, as I've got enough to worry about as it is.

One of my worries centers on my home-office printer, which abruptly begins to act up just weeks after I thought I'd put my printer problems to rest with the replacement cartridge from Japan/Illinois. The display panel tells me I'm encountering an error, which is pretty obvious, since the printer doesn't make a sound when I send things its way. Then the error message disappears altogether, which seems more ominous still.

One afternoon I summon the courage to ask Kevin to begin printing out pages for me at his office again. He rolls his eyes, but he does not say no, which is good enough for me. By now I do not expect such service to come with a smile.

I take a humbling trip to the mall to get my Italian sunglasses repaired. The trip is humbling because for months I have assumed that my sunglasses were so special, so *Italian*, that few eyeglass stores outside of Milan, Italy, would dare to attempt to pop the lens back into the ornate frame. Most of the time I don't even use the word *sunglasses* to describe my sunglasses; I call them my Romeo Giglios, or sometimes just my Romeos, in deference to the Italian fashion designer who created them. For weeks, I've stuck my face behind Kevin's glacier glasses and ignored curious looks in my direction, thinking I had no choice in a world where sunglass options run to extremes: decadently expensive Italian or American ones or cut-rate Chinese ones.

So it's a real surprise when a young woman at the Lenscrafters at the mall, across the corridor from a cafeteria restaurant and around the corner from Sears, takes a quick look at my broken Italian sunglasses and tells me she'll have them ready for me in 10 minutes.

Ten minutes later, she hands them back to me.

"No charge," she says.

I restrain myself and do not leap over the glass counter to embrace her. For this painless episode I have endured glacier-glasses headaches and stoplight stares? I kick myself all the way to the car. I kick myself, but I do not squint. I have restored my Italian sunglasses, my Romeos, to their rightful place, on the front of my face.

I try not to think of Christmas, which is probably the wrong approach because I need to get busy with shopping, and also because it's nearly impossible not to think about Christmas. The stack of toy catalogs stuffed into the mail slot grows thicker each day. Among the catalogs is one that sells expensive toys made mostly in Europe, including handmade wood-and-cotton dolls from Germany that sell for upwards of $100 apiece. I pore through it to see if the company sells light swords, toy police paraphernalia, or anything as tacky as a Morphibian. It does not.

Even the news is unsettling lately. Auto parts maker Delphi files for bankruptcy and is cutting thousands of American jobs, in part because of competition from far cheaper Chinese labor. Meanwhile, China sends two astronauts into space. I don't begrudge China this milestone but I wish there was some good news from home to latch onto. American textile workers continue to reel from job cuts driven by market encroachment by Chinese factories. The most cheering domestic news I've encountered in weeks was a strangely comforting story about a Bigfoot conference in Texas that drew hundreds of attendees.

My mother steps up her needling of me. She tells me that she recently purchased a sleeping bag for Wes and that she cut off the tag that said *Made in China*.

"So you have nothing to worry about," she says.

If only that were true.

■ ■ ■

The week of Halloween I make a trip to the craft superstore and come home with red, gold, and blue fabric from Korea and an American pattern for making children's capes. I find old German thread in a kitchen cabinet. I spend the better part of the day hunched over my sewing machine, pinching my finger in the machine just once.

At day's end I present the children with the finished results: a blue-and-gold prince's costume for Wes, complete with a fabric-covered crown made of cardboard, and a Little Red Riding Hood cape for

Sofie. If a person were to look closely enough they would find unintentional zigs and zags along the hemlines, but I benefit from an uncritical audience and the use of shiny fabrics that hide my wobbly stitches and my inability, despite years of trying, to move beyond advanced-beginner status as a seamstress.

Wes wears his prince's costume to the store, where he draws approving glances from other shoppers who, like the children, appear uncritical of uneven hemlines or suspect puckering at the shoulder seams. Even Kevin seems pleased by Wes's outfit, despite the fact that, technically, his only son is wearing gold lamé to celebrate the holiday.

Kevin and I are invited to a grown-up Halloween party. Costumes are not required, but Kevin wears a black pageboy wig that makes him look like Sonny Bono without the mustache. We've had the wig for years, and just before Kevin slips it onto his head I look inside the synthetic scalp. *Made in China*, it says.

At the party, I tell a friend I haven't seen in ages the story of Wes's purple pumpkin. I realize, midway through my story, that she looks like she is going to cry.

"Poor Wes," she says. She pauses, then asks: "Would you be offended if I brought over some old toys for your kids? I just feel so sorry for them."

I laugh and tell her that's fine, but that, really, Wes is fine.

"I swear he's doing okay," I tell her.

She looks unconvinced.

I forget about this conversation until a couple of mornings later when I step outside the front door and encounter a mound of toys at the foot of our steps. There is a handwritten note taped to a box containing a Barbie doll. It says:

"Our hurricane shelter closed and all of the toys and things they hadn't used were left behind. I couldn't find another shelter that needed this last box. Can your kids have fun with all kinds of things from China that magically appeared at their door? Feel free to call me and have me pick it up for the Goodwill box. I would have done that myself but I thought of that purple pumpkin and well . . . XO, Caroline."

I quickly move most of the toys into the back of the Toyota, where I cover them with a plastic tarp. Then I take a rushed look at what's there. There are plastic animals and soldiers by the hundred, a set of fake gas masks, toy cars, a box containing what claims to be an amphibious school bus, several Barbies, a Lincoln Log set, and dozens of pieces of white dollhouse furniture painted with flowers. I sift through it quickly, worried that the children will wander out of the house and fall in love with the whole lot. I take out the things I think they will like best: the Lincoln Logs, the amphibious school bus, the dollhouse furniture, some felt pens, and some plastic animals. I leave the toy soldiers behind, not due to an antiwar platform but because there is no human foot bottom so calloused that it cannot be pierced by the hard plastic rifle of a toy soldier. I do a fast inventory of the origins of my selections. Everything is made in China.

I step back into the living room with the Chinese bounty for the children, who rip into it with greedy hands. I get a cool response from Kevin after I explain that the toys are unwanted leftovers from a local shelter.

"Well, that's just great," he says. "We've become a charity for deprived children."

■ ■ ■

You hope love lasts forever, but that is not always the case. Certainly Wes's love for the electric purple pumpkin does not endure. The two of them don't even make it through the first week of November.

He seems less enchanted with the pumpkin each day leading up to Halloween, and by two days after the holiday he is so blasé about it that he doesn't object when Sofie hauls it around the house plugging it in and out of wall sockets. She keeps her arms wrapped around it possessively, but Wes doesn't seem to mind.

"Don't you like your pumpkin anymore?" I finally ask.

He shrugs.

"It's okay," he says, eyes not budging from the television set. "I guess."

He *guesses* the electric purple pumpkin is *okay*? For this I sold myself out?

Well, that's it. Never again. No more compromises. No more Chinese toys. No more Chinese anything. No more bent and broken boycott rules, no matter the tears, the pleas, the dirty looks from Kevin. I will face the two months of the boycott's home stretch with the zeal of the recently converted and achieve what the boycott has lacked all year: perfection.

CHAPTER

ELEVEN

The China Season

"I don't have a fallback plan," Kevin says. "This was my fallback plan."

He has called with bad news. The fleece sleeping bags that he wanted to order for the kids for Christmas were made in China.

I tell Kevin that I'm sorry to hear about the sleeping bags, and then I wait for him to tell me that I don't have to say I'm sorry because it's not my fault. He doesn't say that, probably because as architect of the China boycott it is my fault. He also may be thinking that if I were really sorry I'd tell him it's okay for him to go ahead and order the Chinese sleeping bags. It's quiet on his end of the line, meaning he's in a really lousy mood.

I try to cheer him up.

"A lot of the fleece at the craft store is from Korea," I say. "It made me think you had a real shot at those sleeping bags."

He's quiet a little longer, probably trying to make me suffer. Then, when he speaks, he's back to regular Kevin, nice guy with an edge.

"You know what I'm going to do? I'm going to make the kids

sleeping bags," he says. "I'll make them with zippers and Korean fleece. They'll be better than any Chinese sleeping bag you can get from a catalog."

Kevin can build wooden boats and acoustic guitars but as far as I know he can't stitch a button back onto a pair of pants. Not if his life depended on it. I feel compelled to interrupt his surge of good feeling with the warning that I have always found zippers a bit tricky.

"How hard can it be?" he scoffs. "You just sew them on."

The advanced beginner seamstress in me bristles. Kevin pauses.

"Of course, I'm going to need your help," he adds.

"I don't want to help," I say. "I want to watch."

There's another pause.

"Maybe I'll just use Velcro," he says.

■ ■ ■

Probably I should be more sympathetic to Kevin's early miss with the catalog sleeping bags. I, too, have begun the process of calling catalogs to try to decipher if anything on Wes's list to Santa comes from anyplace other than China. It's dreary work and mostly I strike out with my calls. In fact, to date I have struck out every time, since so far every toy I've called about has been made in China.

The calls follow a predictable pattern. I dial the catalog number, ask for the country of origin on a particular item, listen for a sigh or other sign of irritation on the part of the harried customer-service rep, then thank them and hang up after they tell me the toy is made in China. These calls have become so tedious that I am grateful for any deviation from the norm, including the odd exchange that takes place on the day I call to inquire about an Air Power Rocket that can shoot a foam projectile 400 feet into the air.

"Great fun for ages eight and up," the catalog says.

Good way to shoot your eye out, I think.

Mentally, I scratch the rocket from Wes's list as soon as I read about its firepower, but I call about it anyway because I'm curious to know what country makes this potentially eye-destroying plaything. That's how I end up on the phone with Kenneth, a talkative fellow who demonstrates exceptional enthusiasm for my call but cannot tell me where the Air Power Rocket is made.

"No idea!" he exclaims. "What a question!"

Kenneth tells me that he'll have to fill out a form for me and submit it to a "specialist" at the catalog if I want to know where the Air Power Rocket is made. He says someone will call me back with the information in one to three business days. We start to fill out the form, a process that seems routine until I give him the name of our city. That's when Kenneth reveals what I suspect is an unfortunate tendency to tell customers more about himself than they'd probably like to know.

"I spent a night in your town once," he says. "Not that I remember much. Ha, ha, ha. I'm not going to tell that story, no way. *Way* too crazy, even if I could remember all of it. Ha, ha, ha."

As we continue filling out the form Kenneth keeps dropping hints of his wild night in our town, repeating several times that he is definitely not going to tell me about it, no matter what, as if I've been pleading with him to do precisely that. I try to be noncommittal to keep him focused on the form.

"Yeees, Ma'am, that was one wild time," he says. "Area code?"

I give him the number.

"Uh, uh, nooo way, no can do," Kenneth says. "Phone number?"

I hear a buzzing background noise on his end of our connection and Kenneth has to ask me more than once which catalog I'm calling about, which seems like a strange question in that it suggests to me that he isn't sure where he works. I picture Kenneth sitting in some immense call center in South Dakota or Nebraska, surrounded by men and women who used to work in factories that paid union wages but have been downgraded to customer service and $7.50 an hour by competition from Chinese manufacturing plants. Maybe some of those plants, long ago, or maybe not so long ago, used to make some of the toys I'm calling about that are sold in the catalog and that now come, almost certainly, from China.

I am tempted to ask Kenneth if my speculation about his workplace is anywhere near the mark but something stops me. I realize that if I give Kenneth any encouragement whatsoever he'll probably keep me on the phone all afternoon with a detailed description of his work life, from what he thinks of his boss and how much he makes to what sort of decorations he's got on the walls of his cubicle. Somehow along the way I am sure he will work in his sketchy memories of his lost night in our town.

It's not that I wouldn't like to humor Kenneth. It's not even that I've got more important things to do. My objection is practical. I'm in a hurry this afternoon. I've got to make catalog calls about a sno-cone maker and a blue robot if I want to stick to my schedule for sorting through Wes's Chinese Christmas list.

I feel like a heel as I bid good-bye to Kenneth. Would it have killed me to listen to his tale of bacchanalia? It would have been the kind thing to do, and I suspect Kenneth will soon need as much kindness as he can get. I say this because as I hang up I feel certain that Kenneth will soon be fired from his job at the call center for trying to engage customers like me in inappropriate conversations about his youthful misdeeds.

It's a pity Kenneth doesn't have more discretion. Answering the phones for a catalog probably isn't anybody's idea of a dream job, but in an era of rampant offshoring of American jobs to China it could be Kenneth's best shot at gainful employment.

Poor Kenneth. I hope they wait until after the holidays to give him the ax.

No one ever calls me back from Kenneth's company.

■ ■ ■

Another catalog call is also memorable. The woman who answers informs me in a tremulous voice that I will have to send my request to a lawyer named Mr. Klein if I want country-of-origin information on the set of giant cardboard blocks on page 13 of the holiday catalog. She gives me an address in Grandview, Missouri, but tells me I'll get a faster response if I send Mr. Klein a letter by fax. She says she has no idea how long it will take for him to get back to me and asks me if I want the fax number. I write it down.

I never get around to sending a letter to Mr. Klein. It seems like too much trouble. Instead, I abandon the idea of purchasing the cardboard blocks, which would have made a fine present for Sofie, even if they do not appear on her list to Santa.

■ ■ ■

One evening, Wes yanks his list to Santa off the front of the fridge and announces that he wants to write a new one. He throws himself onto his stomach on the kitchen floor and props his chin in his palms. He asks me to recopy his list onto a new piece of paper and instructs me to read out the items on his old list. He says he needs to decide which things to keep on the new list, in case he's changed his mind about what he really wants.

"I will say yes or no," he tells me.

We begin.

Superhero backpack?

He narrows his eyes and looks off across the kitchen, like he's thinking this one over carefully and it's a tough call. "Yes," he says.

Superhero stuff inside the backpack?

He keeps his eyes squeezed half-closed in a sort of meditative state. "Yes."

Light sword?

No hesitation. "Yes!"

A real metal hook with a rope?

"Yes."

Yoyo?

"Yes."

Sword?

"Yes."

Shield?

"Yes."

Lego motorcycle?

"Yes."

I'm relieved to hear it, since a Lego motorcycle sounds like the only possibly non-Chinese item on the list so far.

Fire truck to ride in?

"Yes."

Wagon cart?

"Yes."

Air Power Rocket?

"Yes," he says.

Sorry, kid, I think. Not a chance. I write it down anyway. We'll fight the battle of the Air Power Rocket some other day.

Sky Shark?

"Yes."

Morphibian?

"Yes."

Vampire fangs?

"Yes."

Lunch box?

"Yes."

Monster truck?

"Yes."

Stuffed bear?

"Yes."

Sno-cone maker?

"Yes."

Police badge?

He stops to think this one over. "No," he says slowly, without conviction.

Police hat?

He shakes his head. "No," he says, this time with authority. "Don't want one."

Locker?

"Yes."

Whistle that goes around your neck?

"Yes."

Handcuffs?

A pause and thoughtful squeezing of the eyes. "Yes."

Sunglasses?

"Yes."

Robots? A blue one and all the other colors, too?

"Yes."

I frown at the new list. It appears to be almost identical to the old one, except for the deletions of the police badge and hat, which I will not miss, since surely they are made in China. Wes gets up from the floor and comes to stand by my knee. He asks me to add a couple of additional items from the new toy catalog that's been lying by his side on the floor.

"A monster truck with mote katrol," he says.

He holds up the catalog. He's got the monster truck circled for me.

"And a mote katrol race car," he says. "Tell Santa I really need one of those."

I am missing something. *Mote katrol?* I go blank. Is this something new for the modern child? Am I in danger of becoming like my mother, oblivious to mainstays of contemporary childhood such as Scooby-Doo? Or like my father, who recently brought back a poster of the American cartoon *The Simpsons* as a souvenir of a trip to Sweden?

Mote katrol, I repeat to myself. Then I get it: *remote control.* I add the monster truck and the race car to the list, not that it will do Wes any good. Last time I checked, remote-controlled toys were as Chinese as Mao.

■ ■ ■

I let the children stay home from school after they wake up with runny noses. They sit in a trance in front of the television for most of the morning, and then I drag them to the drugstore for cold medicine.

A Chinese Christmas is in full display. We entertain ourselves pressing the button on a dancing Frosty the Snowman from China, then spend several minutes looking at labels on the undersides of miniature Christmas trees, candleholders in the form of ceramic houses, and other yuletide fare, all made in China. I think maybe Wes is proving to be a precocious child and teaching himself to read because each time we examine a label together he shakes his head and solemnly announces that it is from China. Then he hands me a metal tin with a candle in it that says *Made in Hong Kong* on the bottom.

"Another one from China," Wes sighs.

I bite my tongue.

Wes makes me promise that next year he can buy a miniature Christmas tree with tiny colored ornaments on it. He turns to Sofie with the good news.

"Mama says I can get this when the China season comes," he tells her, holding up the tree. She looks impressed.

It's a pleasant way to pass the time with the children, and there is just one alarming moment.

"*Oh, no!*" I hear Wes exclaim.

I jump and take a few steps down the aisle toward him, thinking maybe he's cut his hand on something. I look for blood but see none. Wes is holding the box of cold medicine in his hand and peering intently at the writing on the outside of it.

"This scared me because I thought it might be from China," he says as he hands it to me. I check the box of cold medicine and find a Rhode Island address. Not from China, I assure him.

We leave the store with the cold medicine and a box of American Kleenex. At least for now you can still blow your nose without China.

■ ■ ■

More notes on a China boycott:

A friend of ours stops her minivan in the street one afternoon and waves me over to the driver's side window.

"My thirteen-year-old daughter is giving up stuff made in China for you," she says. "I thought you'd like to know. And that's on top of Wal-Mart, which she also gave up for you. She adores you."

I'm not sure what to say. Thank you? That's nice? *Is* it nice? Nobody has ever given up Wal-Mart or China for me before, at least not of his or her free will. I'm still trying to figure out what to say when my friend winds up her window and continues down the street.

I order a box of German Christmas toys from a fancy children's catalog. I am shocked when the box arrives. What shocks me is the size of the box. It's no larger than a shoebox, although I spent close to $200 for its contents.

My order seemed enormous and decadent when I called the catalog, but as I unpack the box it all looks dinky and unimpressive. These toys are charming, in good taste, and well made, but as I look them over it dawns on me that these same qualities might count against them from the point of view of the children, who like toys that are loud, large, and in questionable taste; in other words, ordinary toys, which means Chinese toys. And, as I mentioned, these toys are so *small*. The family of four hand-painted dolls from Germany that cost $80 could fit inside a coffee cup. The father doll can't be more than five inches tall. There is also a set of tiny German dollhouse furniture and even tinier German dollhouse accessories, including a toaster and other kitchen utensils that are practically microscopic.

There are other unpleasant surprises in the box. A wooden bathtub boat that the customer-service rep assured me was made in Poland says something else on the outside of its box: *Made in China.*

It hits me that I've spent nearly one third of our holiday budget on this one shoebox worth of toys. I recently suggested to Kevin that we cap our holiday spending at $681 after I read someplace that NPD Group, a retail research firm, predicts the average American family will spend that amount on gifts during the holidays. We are an average enough family in my opinion, although at this point we are not typical, since the typical American family will be spending most of its $681 on Chinese Christmas presents that will thrill their typical American children on the morning of December 25.

It seemed like a sinful amount at the time, but suddenly I'm worried that it will be tough going to keep from busting through the $681 spending cap. After all, the little box had only two things for Wes: the wooden boat from Poland/China, which I'm now going to have to return, and a second wooden boat, made in Germany, powered by rubber bands. In other words, I've just burned through close to 30 percent of our Christmas budget and Wes still faces the prospect of next to nothing under the tree, including not a single thing powered by "mote katrol." Not only that, after looking over my order of German merchandise, I realize that what I really need are *large*, non-Chinese gifts for the children, which I suspect will be even harder to find than small ones.

There is also the matter of friends and relatives who will be sending us gifts, and presumably hoping that we will send something to them, although I prefer not to think about that now. I've got enough on my hands as it is.

I start to feel sorry for myself, so I call my mother, hoping she will feel sorry for me, too.

"I certainly hope you aren't thinking about skimping on toys for the children," she says after I complain that I'm spending too much money with little to show for it so far. "After all, it's been a long year for them and they've been so . . ."

My mother stops short. I finish her sentence for her.

"Deprived?" I ask. "You can say it."

"I didn't use that word," she says. "You did."

It's true that she did not actually say the word, but I could hear her anyway, loud and clear.

■ ■ ■

I buy my second pair of shoes of the year, a pair of suede flats from Brazil that cost $29. My total shoe spending for the year so far, not counting tax and shipping, comes to $39 for this pair and the $10 Israeli desert boots that I bought months ago from the vegan shoe warehouse.

I don't know what will happen in the coming weeks, when panic-driven Christmas spending for large, presumably German toys may clobber us, but the boycott has saved me a small fortune by putting so many pairs of Chinese shoes beyond my reach.

■ ■ ■

I locate an excellent, large, non-Chinese gift for Wes. I pin my hopes on something called a PlasmaCar, a modernistic, ride-on car that is powered by gravity and centrifugal force and holds up to 200 pounds, which means I get to ride it, too. I picture us whooping it up as we take turns racing around the house. I ask Kevin what color he thinks Wes will like best.

"Go with the red," he says.

I can't say with absolute conviction that the PlasmaCar is not made in China because I have only seen it on the Internet and haven't had a chance to call for more information. But I feel optimistic about my chances because the firm that makes it is Canadian and highlights the fact with a maple leaf on its web site. So I've got no worries when I call PlasmaCar's Ottawa headquarters on a Monday morning for confirmation that the cars are indeed made in Canada.

"Not Canada," says the woman who answers the phone. "The cars are made in China."

I replace the receiver and spend a few stunned moments sitting at the kitchen table. I let a blanket of gloom settle over me. I turn and look at the wall calendar. Christmas is a little more than a month away. Sofie is in decent shape, toy-wise, even if her presents are small. At least she will have something to unwrap, and she is probably too young to recognize the dinky nature of her collection of sedate German toys.

But I have nothing for Kevin, or my other relatives, and only two bathtub toys for Wes, including the boat from Poland/China that I need to send back. For Wes there will be no light sword, no robot, no handcuffs, no PlasmaCar.

My glance at the calendar forces me to think about another fast-approaching occasion that, like Christmas, generally demands a mountain of Chinese toys. Wes turns five in less than two weeks, which can mean just one thing.

Disaster.

■ ■ ■

"Let's just go take a look," Kevin says. "It might not be so bad."

Kevin thinks we should go shopping for Wes's birthday at the neighborhood location of a regional toy chain. I say we will be wasting our time.

"I've looked at a lot more toys than you have this year," I tell him. "Believe me, you aren't going to find anything but a bunch of stuff from China in there. It's hopeless. Toys come from China, end of story. That's just the way it is."

He persists.

"I say it's worth a look," Kevin says.

I agree to go with him, mostly to provide the emotional support he will need when he discovers for himself just how dire the toy situation is, and also so that I can tell him I told him so. So nobody is more surprised than I am by what happens next. We haven't been inside the store 10 minutes when we start running into the non-Chinese toys that I've spent all year looking for and missing almost every time. Within minutes there are two items in our basket: a slingshot from Thailand and a set of maze books from Israel.

I shouldn't be surprised by our change of luck. Kevin has a knack for bumping into the unexpected. Years ago, on a trip to Hawaii, Kevin and I were swimming in shallow waters when we ended up in the middle of a herd of sea turtles. Kevin bumped into one. I don't know who was more surprised, Kevin or the turtle. When we got back to shore, my sister-in-law rolled her eyes and said, "It's because Kevin was there. Other people go for a swim and see a few fish. You go swimming with Kevin and it turns into a nature documentary."

Kevin has literally run into politicians (well, one politician, the late Senator Paul Simon, who looked frightened when Kevin spied him in an airport and exclaimed "Paul Simon!"), professional wrestlers (okay, one professional wrestler, Sargent Slaughter, who crushed Kevin's fingers in a handshake after an impromptu meeting in a parking lot), rock stars (well, one rock star, Jonathan Richman, who sat down next to him at a bar and maybe isn't a rock star so much as a musician with a cult following), and Eastern European presidents (all right, one anyway, Viktor Yushchenko, the president of Ukraine whose skin turned gray and pockmarked after he was poisoned; Kevin met him on the street last summer in Paris and said the man looked even sicker in person than on television). In the animal world, Kevin has collided with bears and dolphins as well as sea turtles and wild sheep. When you are with Kevin you never know what will happen.

It's a point that applies to our excursion to the toy store, where the items from Thailand and Israel suggest that Kevin is going to save Wes's birthday, which means that he might save Christmas for him, too. And Kevin is just getting started. He asks the salesgirl to let him take a look at a blowgun displayed high on a wall. I think he's pressing his luck.

"That couldn't possibly be from anyplace but China," I say under my breath while the girl goes to get a ladder. "You shouldn't make her climb up there."

The girl hands down the blowgun to Kevin, who takes a close look at the packaging.

"Thailand," he says, and drops it into the basket with a supercilious arch in his brow.

Next he wanders over to look at puzzles. He picks out one with a medieval knight theme and tosses it in the basket.

"American," he smirks.

I start to think maybe there's nothing so hard about a China boycott. Maybe it's just me. Maybe I have bad retail instincts, or bad luck, or Kevin has good instincts and good luck.

Whatever it is, luck or instinct, today it rescues Wes's birthday.

■ ■ ■

Kevin witnesses a fight between snooty ladies at a snooty cook shop where he goes to look for a gadget to help me make pie crusts. He wants to give me the gadget for Christmas.

He doesn't mind snooty shops, either because he's oblivious to the snootiness or because he simply doesn't care about it one way or another, and this visit is no exception. One of the snooty ladies on the staff leads him to the baking section and locates the tool he wants. Then he remembers the boycott and checks the label.

"Sorry," he says. "I can't get it. I am not buying stuff made in China."

The snooty lady has just started to give him a cold look that is the hallmark of such ladies when another snooty lady, this one a customer, sidles by them in the aisle and overhears his comment.

"Good for you," she tells him in the booming voice of one accustomed to having the world at her beck and call. "You can go to Wal-Mart if you want things made by Chinese slave labor. That's not why we come to this place."

I eat this story up.

"And then what did the first snooty lady say, the one that worked there?" I ask Kevin. "How did she come back from that? Was she just dying?"

"She didn't say anything," he says.

"How could she not say anything?" I ask. "She must have said something."

He shrugs. I push for more details. This is a delicious scene— one snooty lady out-snootied by another—and I want the blow-by-blow.

"Well, what was her expression then? Like she had a lemon in her mouth? Was she mad?"

Another shrug.

"Did you all just stand there looking at each other?" I ask next.

"I just walked away," he says. "When I left, they were both just standing there saying nothing."

I lean back with my glass of wine and play this scene over in my head. It would have been nice to have more details, of course. If only I could have been there, too. I really do need a gadget to help me make piecrusts, but I consider this story ample compensation in its place, a tasty bit of revenge against every snooty store clerk that's ever chased me from her shop with dagger eyes. I view it as a gift to me from the China boycott, better than a good piecrust any day and sweeter still because it didn't cost us a thing.

■ ■ ■

My mother uses the occasion of Wes's five-year-old birthday party to demonstrate once again her feeling for the boycott—*my* boycott.

She peels off the *Made in China* label on a Scooby-Doo waffle maker but employs a different technique to alter the outside of the box that contains a Chinese sleeping bag for Wes. She uses a black felt pen to change the printed lettering so that it now reads *Made in Chile*. She's still insisting that I am being difficult and won't accept Chinese gifts, although I have explained on repeated occasions that this is not the case due to the gift exemption.

"Oh, I know how you feel about these things," she says over the phone. "You can't fool me."

All the guests bring Chinese toys to the party, including a superhero backpack and a set of rescue hero toys. I am resigned to this predictable infusion of Chinese products into the house and use the occasion to look on the bright side. I scratch the superhero backpack and superhero stuff from Wes's list to Santa.

Like Israel and Thailand, Mexico helps save the day. Kevin blows up at least 100 Mexican balloons and scatters them about the house. The children use a bat to destroy a Mexican piñata in the shape of a dinosaur. This time, we even send the guests home with party bags containing Danish Lego trucks. Wes is thrilled with his haul of toys, and is particularly fond of the Thai slingshot, which he uses to pelt his sister with foam balls when we are not looking.

So we end November on a high note. Almost a high note, anyway.

On the last night of November, with Christmas hovering like a ghoul, Wes reminds me that all is not well, and that this is no time to rest on the laurels of his birthday.

"It's almost Christmas, Mama," he says, as I tuck him into bed. "That means Santa's coming soon and he's going to bring me everything I want. Even a light sword."

TWELVE

Road's End

I have already sucked my candy cane into a fragile dagger of red and white sugar when I think to look at the ruins of the candy box scattered beside me on the sofa.

It's an impromptu decision. I don't know why I do it. There is no logical reason for bargain candy canes to come from China. And I am not even thinking about the boycott. I am enjoying watching the children hang candy canes from the low-lying branches of our Christmas tree and wondering if our dog, Rick, who has a sweet tooth and isn't deterred by plastic wrappers, will sneak them from the branches in the coming days. It's a rare moment when I don't have China on the brain. So maybe it's just habit when I reach for the torn box resting a few inches from my hand, pick it up, and turn it over.

Peppermint stings my mouth as I read the label. I sit up and stare at the words. *Made in China.* You have *got* to be kidding me.

I thought I'd seen it all, or at least pretty close to it. Chinese toys, Chinese shoes, Chinese tools, more Chinese toys, Chinese electronics,

Chinese luggage, Chinese designer clothes worthy of Gwyneth Paltrow, and then more Chinese toys—these I have come to expect. But Chinese candy canes from the drugstore at 99 cents a dozen? I never expected to see them, not here in our living room, not now, in the waning days of the boycott.

I thought we'd become experts on avoiding Chinese merchandise. I thought we had learned a few things since January and that we could eke out a short streak of boycott perfection as we race toward the finish line. The Chinese candy canes suggest otherwise. We're still amateurs, even at this late hour, clueless to the lurking Chinese merchandise in the drugstore and negligent about checking labels. I pause. I am being too hard on myself. I should say that the Weakest Link is still an amateur. After all, the candy canes were Kevin's idea. He thought they might liven up the sad tree twinkling with old Chinese lights in the corner of our living room.

"Hey, Kev," I call into the kitchen now. "Can I show you something?"

Kevin saunters out of the kitchen with a dish towel over his shoulder and a dusting of flour across the front of his T-shirt from baking cookies with the kids. He frowns at the empty box that I brandish before him, then a wave of disbelief sweeps over him as he gets my meaning. He's already pale from too little sun. Now he seems to go one shade lighter.

"No," he says. "I don't believe it. You're putting me on."

I give him an arch look.

"If only that were the case," I say.

"A confection? From China?" he says with an odd formality that makes him sound British. "I had no idea. I didn't even think to look at the box."

Obviously, I think.

"You can't be too careful," I say, "especially around the holidays."

He shakes his head and returns to the kitchen, muttering to himself.

"Who would think that a Christmas confection would come from China?" I hear him ask the four walls of the room.

Not me. Not the Weakest Link either. Not in a million years.

■ ■ ■

I trace Kevin's bungle with the Chinese candy canes to an ironic source: too much confidence in his own China-dodging abilities. Sure, he's been getting into the spirit of things recently, but he's also getting cocky and careless. He's become a boycott show-off. I know what goes before a fall—pride—but Kevin forgets that rule of thumb each time he returns home to dangle more non-Chinese Christmas merchandise in front of me, a sly smile on his face. Kevin is better at boycotting China than I am and is making sure I don't miss that fact.

Consider his trip to the toy store earlier today. With just 22 shopping days left until Christmas, he wanders into the same toy store where he had such good luck for Wes's birthday. Half an hour later he strolls back out the door with a T-ball set from Thailand, a Tumblin' Monkeys game from Romania, a set of glow-in-the-dark ceiling stickers shaped like stars and made in Uruguay, and some more maze books from Israel. From Taiwan there is a set of colorful foam swords and a hard, round disk that expands into a towel with a dinosaur theme after you soak it in water.

He is puffed up like a rooster as he unloads his shopping bag at the kitchen table so I can look over the spoils.

"I can't believe it," I say, more to myself than to him. "How do you find this stuff?"

"Nothing to it," he tells me. "Things work best when you just relax and let the non-Chinese toys find you. You can't try too hard. You have to let it happen."

I feel a little jealous. Well, okay, a lot jealous. Kevin's stack of non-Chinese toys includes large, colorful toys that the children might actually play with, in contrast to my shoebox of sedate and tasteful German gifts. I spent nearly $200 on the contents of that tiny box. I take a look at the receipt from Kevin's shopping excursion. For $93 he has Wes's Christmas locked up, large toys included.

I could mention to Kevin that foam swords from Taiwan are not the same as battery-operated light swords from China. Foam swords cannot actually harm anyone. I think you can safely assume that nobody has ever lost an eye to a foam sword. I am not sure you could say the same thing about genuine, hard-plastic light swords. Nor do safe, bendable foam swords appear anywhere on Wes's wish list to Santa, an additional factor that could diminish their allure to Wes on Christmas morning. I also keep quiet about the fact that Wes took one look at the Israeli maze books he received for his birthday, tossed them to the side, and hasn't picked them up since, suggesting that these latest maze books also may be duds.

If I had a mind to do it I could also tell Kevin that if he is anticipating a big hurrah from Wes over the expanding dinosaur towel from Taiwan he may want to think again. The packaging calls it a towel but its finished dimensions suggest it will be closer to a washcloth after it has expanded to its full size, a point that won't slip by Wes unnoted.

I also do not see anything in Kevin's bag with a superhero theme, anything with wheels, or anything powered by remote control. There is no sign of Scooby-Doo or robots and not a single thing that makes a noise, from which I conclude that, while China will be missing from Wes's Christmas morning, lots of other things will be missing, too.

I take the high ground. I let Kevin have his fun. I keep my thoughts to myself. I tell myself that, sooner or later, the boycott will knock him back down to size and he'll learn through painful experience, as I have, that China owns Christmas, a pair of Taiwanese foam swords and a few lucky breaks from Israel and Uruguay notwithstanding. I know it will be a humbling moment for Kevin when it comes, as it inevitably will.

Kevin's humbling moment comes sooner than expected. It comes tonight, just hours after his jubilant return from the toy store, when I absentmindedly reach for the carcass of the candy cane box and uncover the truth about China moving into the business of Christmas candies.

Or, as Kevin calls them, confections.

■ ■ ■

It is the first of several diminishing moments in the weeks before Christmas.

To begin, we discover that the plastic knight figurine that came inside the box that contained Wes's supposedly American birthday puzzle was made in China. It's too late to return the puzzle. Wes has already begun losing puzzle pieces, including one that he squeezed into a crack in the stairwell leading to the upstairs bedrooms. He did not take the news well when I explained that it would have to remain there forever.

The screen of the television freezes up while Kevin and I are in the middle of a murder mystery. We pump the remote control at the DVD player from a dozen angles but nothing gets the movie going again. The interruption forces us to leave an English aristocrat dangling from his wrists with a gag over his mouth and a killer on the loose while Kevin rushes to RadioShack to see if he can get a new remote control or a repair of the old one. While he's standing in line, he sees stacks of new Chinese DVD players on sale for $29.

"It's not the remote," the man at RadioShack tells Kevin. "You need a new DVD player."

Kevin leaves the store empty-handed.

The outcome of this episode is hardly disastrous. After Kevin gets home we discover that the DVD player still works, it just doesn't respond to the remote control, meaning we have to get up and down off the sofa to press its buttons manually. For a few days Kevin makes bitter remarks about the $29 DVD players from China ("It's like they were taunting me," he says), but his bile ebbs away and after that he doesn't mention the matter again.

Wes is invited to another birthday party. He brings Legos as a gift. The party takes place at an art studio where a woman shows the children how to draw a picture of something chosen by the birthday boy. When Wes gets home he shows me his drawing of a fire-breathing beast with wings and a serpentine tail.

"It's a Chinese dragon," he says. "Dragons live in China."

It's Wes's best drawing ever. I tack the dragon to the kitchen wall and try to ignore the feeling that it is watching the back of my head as I do the dishes.

A box from a company called Soaps Gone Buy of Harrisburg, Illinois ("Where soaps of yesterday are found TODAY!"), appears on our front steps one afternoon. The box is addressed to Kevin, who has already told me to expect it and what it contains: 10 bars of Fels-Naptha soap, as a Christmas present for me. The soap is made in the USA, can obliterate almost any stain, is probably poisonous, possibly flammable, and lasts more or less forever. We bought a single bar of Fels-Naptha soap about 15 years ago and I only threw out the last sliver of that original bar a couple of months ago, when it had become too skinny to grip.

I stare at the Soaps Gone Buy label on the box and try to let the reality of what has happened sink in. My husband, the man who once brought me flowers, Italian underwear, and French pajamas, has just purchased 150 years' worth of possibly poisonous soap for me as a Christmas gift.

It's not even a surprise.

■ ■ ■

A letter to the editor catches my eye as I scan the local paper.

"Forget Chinese; remember Christmas," declares the headline. The writer begins with a brief description of ill-behaved holiday shoppers and then homes in on his central complaint: China is taking over Christmas.

I could have told him that.

"Today it's not American workers and factories that are benefiting from the Christmas season, it's our enemy, communist 'Red' China. . . . For the Chinese, it's a time to celebrate the accumulation of more American wealth," Jim A. writes. "For reasons inexplicable, we have given the communist Chinese complete and total access to our consumer markets. . . . Only a few months ago, the Chinese bought into IBM. They were also casting their eyes on UNOCAL and Maytag. This is only the beginning of red Chinese business ventures into America."

Next Jim A. laments, "Santa Claus has been outsourced to China." He urges readers to remember the religious significance of the holiday and states that to do otherwise is to face eternal damnation.

Jim A.'s letter unnerves me, on several counts. First, I get a little edgy when somebody starts name-dropping Jesus, who is big on forgiveness, while at the same time tossing around the word "enemy." My mother would have lots to say on this point but she's not here, so I move on to my second gripe regarding the letter: red-baiting.

China is not a democracy—far from it, and I agree it's a pity—but does Jim A. really have to call the Chinese *reds*? It's not that they aren't red, but calling them red is petty name-calling, something naughty children do on the playground but eventually outgrow, or at least you hope they outgrow it.

Not only that, *reds* sounds so out-of-date, the linguistic equivalent of a woman who still wears a beehive hairdo 40 years after it went out of fashion. It suggests an unwillingness to accept that the world is changing, or that it was far from perfect to begin with. Jim A. has doomed himself to disappointment if he expects the nation's holiday shoppers to behave well in crowded malls or to remember the true meaning of Christmas when they are buffeted by crass commercial demands, such as those made by five-year-old boys who make no secret of their wish to own *mote katrol* monster trucks that, I remind you, Jim A., come from China.

I also feel it's impolite to tell strangers they will be going to hell if they don't rein in their spending on Chinese merchandise, and quick.

Something else eats at me as I look over the letter, something bigger and more troubling. It is the fact that, for better or for worse, I am currently doing precisely what angry, red-baiting, name-calling Jim A. is urging everybody else to do: keeping my hands off Chinese merchandise for the holidays.

Jim A. and I seem to have little in common. I don't consider the Chinese to be my enemies. I've never called anybody a *red*. I was raised by peaceniks in California. Jim A. hails from the Bible Belt. We're even boycotting China for different reasons. With him, it's personal. Red China offends Jim A.'s sensibilities, whereas I like to tell myself that our family boycott is an objective experiment in globalization. Sure, I have my China-is-taking-over-the-world panic attacks, especially in the toy aisle, especially before Christmas, but at heart our boycott isn't personal. Why, I like to think it's practically *scientific*. And yet, at this juncture in the nation's pre-Christmas frenzy of spending on Chinese merchandise, I'm probably as close to a model citizen as Jim A. is going to get.

I don't like that one bit.

Recently, I've been considering what my friend asked me not long ago, about whether we were going to reunite with China after the boycott comes to a finish on December 31. Jim A.'s letter pushes me in the direction of a reunion with China, if only to spite him, and to prove, if only to myself, that I am not a thing like him. That decision will come later, in consultation with the Weakest Link, who I am certain will wave China back through the front door like an old friend.

In the meantime, I will continue to do what Jim A. insists every American should be doing but apparently almost no one is. I will avoid Chinese Christmas gifts as if my salvation depended on it, which, in his view, it does.

■ ■ ■

"Don't look inside the bag," Kevin barks. "I've got some presents for you in there."

I am momentarily bewildered. The bag he's just swung onto the kitchen table is from Office Depot. There must be some mistake. Copy paper comes from Office Depot. Printer cartridges come from Office Depot. Pens come from Office Depot. Christmas presents from Kevin to me do not come in Office Depot bags, or at least they never have before.

"Do you mean there's another bag from someplace else inside the Office Depot bag?" I ask. "A bag with perfume, or earrings in it? A book? A scarf?"

Kevin isn't listening. He's whistling under his breath and unpacking the Office Depot bag.

"I've got miniature staplers for the kids from Germany, marker pens from Italy, colored highlighters from I don't know where but not China, and some Office Depot brand tape made, I think, in the USA," he says.

He holds up each item as he goes along.

"And then there are a couple of things for you, including something made in Canada that's still out in the car, something big. So that makes three things for you."

Three Christmas presents for me from Office Depot? I can't think of even one thing from Office Depot that I would like to have for Christmas, unless Office Depot has overhauled its inventory and now stocks perfume, earrings, scarves, and books on subjects other than personnel management.

Kevin reaches into the bag and extracts a German-made pencil sharpener.

"Precision engineered," he says.

He holds up a package of Post-It notes.

"Made right here in the US of A," he says.

Kevin is in high spirits. Never in Office Depot's history have its products made anyone happier. I take in the growing pile of office products on the kitchen table with a wan smile, trying to keep the hangdog dread out of my eyes.

"One of the things I got for you didn't have any information on it about where it was made, not on the box or on the thing itself, but I got it anyway," Kevin says. He looks up and points a finger at me: "Because you can't prove a negative."

My heart has been sinking but this last claim perks me up a bit.

A little snottily, I ask, "Who says you can't prove a negative?"

"Science," Kevin says. He has started to return the Christmas office supplies to the bag.

"Are you sure?" I ask. "Isn't it that you can't prove a positive and that you can *only* prove a negative? Or is it disprove a positive? I think that's it."

Kevin likes a lively debate. Normally, he would take the bait right here. He would start by reminding me that he got an A in college philosophy and then we would go back and forth on the nature of scientific theories until we agreed to call my older brother, the marine biologist, to let him settle it, but today Kevin is in too good a mood. He ignores me and crumples up the top of the Office Depot bag to close it. He winks at me.

"The rest of what's in here is off-limits to you," he says. "Until Christmas morning, that is. I'm going to hide all this in our closet. Promise me you won't look. And don't go peeking into the car either until I can get the thing from Canada out of the back."

I shake my head at him. I am definitely not tempted to go snooping in the Office Depot bag, or the Toyota.

Kevin makes his way down the hall and leaves me with my thoughts, or my one thought, which is that he has never given me either soap or office supplies for Christmas during 17 years of marriage. Then I recall that he's supposed to be giving me piano lessons again this year, which last year translated into no Christmas present at all. No Christmas present at all is starting to sound better all the time, especially if the alternative is soap and Canadian office supplies. Kevin has always been a terrific gift giver, and he has surprisingly good taste in clothing and housewares for a man who has spent the better part of his life in ripped shorts and flip-flops. He doesn't have to go to any of this trouble, since the piano lessons get him off the hook without his ever having to leave the house. What could possibly have gotten into him?

The answer is so obvious that I scold myself for not seeing it right off. What has gotten into him is the China boycott. He is not thinking straight. Either that, or he thinks soap and office supplies make fine gifts at Christmas.

■ ■ ■

My younger brother sends an e-mail from California asking me what he should send the kids for Christmas.

"Tell me what you and Kevin want, too," he writes.

He doesn't actually say, *Make a list and send it my way, chop-chop.* The message is implied.

On its surface this is not an unreasonable request, even if it does come on December 16, which, if you think about it, is late to get started thinking about gifts. My brother wants to get the children something they like for Christmas, rather than leaving the matter to chance and a panicked trip to Toys "R" Us. Fair enough. More than fair, really—kind, even thoughtful. But if that's the case, why is my head getting hot as I read his e-mail again?

I'll tell you why.

I repeat that it is December 16. There is only a little over a week until Christmas. My brother, who has a well-deserved reputation as a last-minute shopper, wants me to provide him with a tidy list of acceptable merchandise so he can set aside 20 minutes of his work day for Internet shopping and get the holidays wrapped up by 5 P.M. Pacific Time. And he wants to use my boycott-addled brain to help him do it, *chop-chop*. But my brain is used up. I've used it up on the sweaty, nervous attempt to participate in the biggest consumer orgy of the year without help from China.

The results of my efforts are mixed. Kevin is getting a pair of Cambodian pants from me, which is only slightly more romantic than the soap and office supplies I will receive from him. From the children Kevin will receive a couple packages of inexpensive Pakistani underwear that I picked up for next to nothing at the liquidation sale of a third-tier department store. It was my bleakest retail experience in recent memory. I had to cut short my underwear shopping when an agitated junkie started to follow me through the aisles. In the boys' department I overheard a large woman with a red face telling her young son she would throw him out of the store if he did *that* again.

Technically, I have come up with gifts for everybody on our list: books that I'm not sure they'll like, T-shirts, fancy foods, that sort of thing. I have alternately spent too much money on some people (my mother will make out with a silk scarf from India that is to die for) and too little on others (my brothers, who will be getting T-shirts from Bangladesh that looked okay in the store but had morphed into limp rags by the time I got home from the mall). I couldn't come up with anything for my dad and ended up getting him a gift certificate, leaving me vulnerable to the possibility that he will use it to purchase something made in China.

The impact of the boycott on my shopping has been subtly detrimental. I have spent so much time and money trying to locate non-Chinese toys for Sofie and Wes that I have scant imagination, and little cash, left over for anybody else.

Not that any of this has stopped me from spending. The other day I ordered an American-made doll cradle for Sofie from the same fancy catalog that sent me the shoebox of small German things. My rationale is ridiculous: I was worried that Sofie wouldn't have anything large under the Christmas tree. That sort of thinking has wreaked havoc on our $681 holiday budget. I would guess we are at least $200 past that point, although I haven't had the courage to sit down and add the receipts. I get dizzy thinking about the money. I won't let myself think about the decadent more-is-better message that we're conveying to the children. I feel sick enough as it is.

None of this is my younger brother's fault. He's oblivious to the pressures of the China boycott since I've reserved most of my belly-aching for Kevin and my mother. My brother is a victim of the boycott in a roundabout way. He doesn't know that it has transformed me into a ball of nerves, ready to lash out at the first person to ask me to pony up a list of toys for the children, and on the double. Nevertheless, his e-mail stings. Doesn't he realize what I've been up against? How can he be so clueless? Can't he see that I have Christmas worries of my own?

So I admit that I am not being fair. And I'm not being fair when I do what I do next. I sit at the keyboard for a few minutes after his e-mail lands in my in-box and I stare at the screen. Then I type out a response.

It starts with a dig. I tell him not to worry about gifts for me and Kevin at this point, meaning it's getting late for that, don't you think? Then I tell him that Wes would love a monster truck with a remote control. A baby doll would be perfect for Sofie. I add a note at the end asking him to make sure the monster truck and the doll don't come from China, and wish him luck. This is a masterstroke of insincerity, and cruel to boot, since the boycott gift exemption gets my brother off the hook with regard to Chinese toys, something he is unlikely to remember in the confused rush of last-minute shopping.

It is nine days before Christmas. I have just asked my brother to do the impossible: find a baby doll and a monster truck from some place other than China. *Chop*-chop.

I am not the sort of person who takes pleasure in the torment of others, at least not until recently. But sometimes you have to have your fun where you find it.

■ ■ ■

When the phone rings a few nights later I sense that something awful has happened as soon as I pick up the receiver.

"It's the Toyota," Kevin says. "It's been stolen. I need somebody to come get me."

The irony hits me instantly and like a ton of bricks: in the final days of the China boycott our car has been stolen from the parking lot of a Chinese restaurant.

Kevin looks dazed after my older brother picks him up and drops him off at our house. We sit on the sofa and he gives me the blow-by-blow of events leading up to the Toyota's disappearance.

The family of one of the graduate students in Kevin's department at the university had invited him to dinner at a Chinese restaurant. Kevin spent about an hour and a half in the restaurant eating spicy chicken and drinking ice water, and when he came out the Toyota was gone. He spent another hour driving around the mall parking lot, first in a cart with a shopping center security guard, and then with a deputy sheriff, looking for the car in the outside chance that he had forgotten where he parked it and had only misplaced it.

"It was just gone," he says.

"Are you sure you didn't just forget where you put it?" I ask.

"Not unless I'm losing my mind, and I mean completely losing my mind because I'm positive about where I left it," Kevin says. "Positive."

He says he is absolute on the Toyota's last known location because when he got to the Chinese restaurant every space in its lot was taken, so he drove across a side street to park in the lot of a seafood restaurant in the same strip center, where there were lots of open spaces. He got out of the Toyota and looked around to see if there was a sign telling him he could only park there if he was going inside to the seafood restaurant or he'd be towed. There was no sign. Next he took a few steps away from the car before turning back to double-check that he'd locked the doors. He had. Then he left, unwittingly bidding good-bye to the Toyota for the last time.

After dinner, he walked back to the seafood restaurant's parking lot. Business must have picked up at the fish place, because this time its lot had just one empty space: the spot where he had parked the Toyota. He walked right back to the space. Then he walked around the lot to make sure he wasn't mistaken, but the car wasn't anywhere to be seen. And he was certain that's where it was supposed to be. He ran it over in his head again and again.

"That's where I left it, but when I got back it was gone," he says. "So unless I'm losing my mind it was stolen."

We sit and rehash the details ad nauseam until nearly midnight, when finally I think to ask him about his dinner. He cheers up.

"Delicious," he says. "I even got a pretty good fortune in my cookie."

He digs into his pocket for the slip of paper so I can read his fortune for myself. "You will have many bright days soon," it says.

Below that it gives a string of lucky numbers: 1, 19, 20, 28, 34, and then, for some reason, the number 20 appears again.

"Wait a second," I say.

I take Kevin's fortune, get up, and walk into the kitchen to check the wall calendar. It is December 19, a lucky day for Kevin, according to his fortune cookie. This is a monumental happening. Two monumental happenings, really. One: we have just had a car stolen for the first time ever, thereby joining the ranks of the faceless millions of property crime victims. Two: I believe we have just blown open a scandal involving the false promises of Chinese fortune cookies.

■ ■ ■

A China boycott does not stop Christmas. A stolen car does not stop Christmas. Nothing stops Christmas. The day after the Toyota goes AWOL we call the insurance company, file some paperwork, and get back to the business of surviving the holidays without Chinese merchandise.

I thought maybe Kevin gave up on the idea of sewing sleeping bags for the kids after he decided to build them wooden lap desks to hold all the office supplies he bought for them at Office Depot. But on December 21, hours after putting the finishing touches on the desks, he asks me to set up the sewing machine at the kitchen table so he can get down to business.

"I'll be right back," he says over his shoulder as he heads for the door. He speeds away to the craft superstore in our one remaining car, the Volkswagen.

I rig the machine with old German thread. Kevin returns in 20 minutes with a plastic bag. Inside are two big pieces of Korean fleece, one with a Scooby-Doo theme and the other with a Winnie-the-Pooh pattern. He's decided to avoid the perils of zippers and rely instead on American-made Velcro that he found at the craft store.

I'm impressed. The craft superstore is *my* stomping ground, not Kevin's. It's an enormous place stocked with endless items, nearly all of them made in China, and none of them arranged in any particular order, as far as I can tell. I don't recall even once seeing a man in the fabric section, where the skeleton crew of ladies can be brusque if you equivocate about how much fabric you need them to cut for you. It can be an intimidating place, especially if you don't know how to sew, probably especially if you are a man who doesn't know how to sew, and potentially even openly hostile if you don't know how much fleece you need for sleeping bags because you don't have a pattern and are just winging it.

"So how did you know how much fleece to ask for?" I ask Kevin.

He looks at me as if this is a silly question.

"I just held my hands apart and told the lady, 'About four times as much as this,'" he says, demonstrating with arms stretched wide.

As Kevin settles in at the machine I find it hard to take him seriously. He's wearing an ancient orange beret that his grandmother crocheted for him in the early 1980s. Before he's even started to sew he asks, "Does fabric have a wrong side and a right side?"

When I'm done disguising my laughter as a cough I help him fold the piece of Scooby-Doo fleece in two and show him how to place pins a few inches apart along the edges. Then I give him a primer on the sewing machine.

"It's like a car," I begin. "Press the pedal to go faster or slower, and take your foot off if you want to stop. There's no brake."

"Got it," he says.

"Watch your fingers, and be sure to take the pins out before you run over them so you don't break the needle."

"Check."

I leave him to it and wander over to the counter, where I pretend to balance the checkbook so I can keep an eye on him.

"I'm going to sew first, then deal with the Velcro," he says to himself.

Lips pursed in concentration, Kevin gingerly presses the pedal and begins slow-motion sewing. I didn't know the machine could go that slow. He makes steady progress along the first edge, and I remark to myself that he's not doing too badly, considering I expected immediate and outright disaster. But Kevin is not a patient crafter. He hasn't yet completed the first long edge of the sleeping bag when he lifts his foot to stop the needle and looks up at me. He is still wearing the orange beret, which has slipped to a jaunty angle.

"Is there any trick to this?" he asks. "I want to get this done and I've already spent fifteen minutes on it."

Kevin gets most of the way through the seams on the first sleeping bag. When he holds it up to look it over I can't help but notice that it looks more like a big fleece burrito than a traditional sleeping bag, not that it will make a bit of difference to the kids or anyone else.

"I can see there's some skill involved with this sewing thing," Kevin says as he inspects his work. "I'm going to finish this later."

■ ■ ■

I had expected controversy this morning, perhaps the result of my getting a little too loose with the ridicule or Kevin getting touchy about his seams. I was ready for an ugly spat involving exchanges through clamped teeth about a lack of mutual support. To my surprise, it's been fun.

Then my mother calls, and controversy begins. It begins almost immediately, after Kevin mentions that he's sewing sleeping bags for the kids. He goes quiet after that. From across the kitchen I hear a distant, tinny squawk coming from my mother's end of the connection. I watch Kevin clench his square jaw, a worrisome sign.

"No, Lois, you never gave our family sleeping bags," he says. "Yes, I'm positive."

His voice is patient and level.

Kevin goes quiet again. Now his lips are getting tense. On and on my mother goes. I look at Kevin and mouth the words, "What is she talking about?"

He covers the receiver with his hand.

"She's insisting that she sent the whole family sleeping bags years ago, on top of the one she just sent Wes for his birthday," he whispers. "She's offended that I'm sewing new ones because she says I must not think the ones she sent were good enough."

"She never gave us sleeping bags," I whisper back to Kevin. "She's losing it."

He puts the phone back to his ear. His voice is still level, even saintly, I would offer, under the circumstances.

"No," he says into the receiver. "You didn't."

He puts his hand over the receiver a second time and relays me her latest accusation.

"Now she says I'm accusing her of not sending us sleeping bags," he says. "She says I'm accusing her of sending sleeping bags to your brothers but not to us in a show of favoritism. She just asked me if I am accusing her of being unfair."

He holds the phone away from his ear at arm's length while my mother continues her rant. Before he puts the receiver back to his ear, Kevin does something that many, maybe most, sons-in-law have done at some point in their lives during interaction with their mothers-in-law but that is a first for him, as far as I know. He rolls his eyes.

When he speaks again Kevin's voice has changed. There's an edge slipping into it. My mother is giving him guff, and if there is one thing in this world that Kevin does not care for, it's guff. My mother has never given Kevin guff in the past and he's not going to start taking it from her at this late date.

"Are you saying it's wrong that I should sew sleeping bags for my family?" he says. "Is that what you are trying to tell me?"

He holds the phone away from his ear again and does something else that he's never done during a conversation with my mother. He grimaces. My mother can't see him, but something tells me she's starting to catch a hint. He puts the phone back to his ear. I can tell that my mother is backing down.

"We can discuss this some other time," Kevin says. He's all business by now, curt and polite.

More distant apologies from my mother.

"That's all right, gotta go," he says, then looks at me. "She's right here."

I fan my hands frantically and mouth the words, *Do not give me the phone.*

"On second thought, not a good time," he says. "I'll have her call you later."

He signs off with my mother and then gives me a withering look, as if I'm to blame for her false memories about sleeping bags past. Kevin removes the orange beret and tosses it on the counter. Sewing did not wear him out, but my mother just did.

"You realize she wouldn't have learned about any of this if we'd just ordered the sleeping bags from the catalog," he says.

"I know," I say. "But they were . . ."

My voice trails off and we leave the next word unspoken. Chinese.

■ ■ ■

Kevin takes a two-day hiatus from sleeping-bag construction. Then, on the morning of December 23, he's back in the kitchen at the machine.

This morning Kevin's beginner's luck runs out early. Not 10 minutes after he's started he breaks the needle on a thick layer of fleece. He gets back in the Volkswagen and heads to a sewing shop that he locates in the phone book. When he gets home again he reports that the little old lady who runs the shop was offended when he asked if the needles he wanted were made in China.

"Germany," she sniffed.

He says she warmed up after that when he told her what he was working on and even inquired about group sewing classes.

Two hours later, he finishes the sleeping bags.

To describe them as beautiful would be to miss the point, and to miss the truth. There are dozens of uncut white threads tangled up in the Velcro, abruptly shifting seam lines, and a raw edge along the side of one of the bags that warns, in large black letters on a white background, "Do not use for children's sleepwear."

Kevin shrugs as he considers the warning, which we had missed until now.

"I think they are talking about pajamas," he says. "It doesn't say anything about sleeping bags."

■ ■ ■

I was wrong when I said we'd seen the last mouse of the year. We encounter the true last mouse, identical to the others, on the afternoon of

Christmas Eve. We could hardly miss it. It runs along the floorboard of the living room in the middle of the day while we are sitting on the sofa watching television.

That afternoon Kevin drives to the pet store with the children, where he asks a clerk whether they sell mousetraps.

"This is a *pet store*, sir," the alarmed young man tells Kevin, his meaning being that pet stores are in the business of helping to keep animals, including mice, *alive*.

Kevin drops in at the hardware store and buys another traditional American trap.

That night we set out cookies for Santa and permit the children to open one present each. They choose the boxes from their uncle in California. For Wes there is an enormous, red monster truck with a remote control. For Sofie there is a baby doll with long blond hair and an empty expression.

I don't waste any time. I retrieve the packaging from the floor so I can inspect the bottom of the toy boxes. Both of them say *Made in China*. So much for my masterstroke of insincerity. My brother sent it back at me, in spades.

After we send the kids to bed we finish wrapping presents in front of the television. This time it's not Mass from the Vatican but a nice choral performance of traditional hymns. Kevin sets the American mousetrap under the sink just before bed. Upstairs, Wes lies awake listening for bells and hooves on the roof. He calls out several times for water and reassurance that Santa's sleigh won't plunge through the roof and crush him while he dreams. He puts the monster truck on the floor next to his bed so he can reach down and touch it during the night to make sure it's still there.

Downstairs, we lie in bed and wait for another sound, the snap of the trap under the sink.

■ ■ ■

The children are out of bed and down the stairs before first light. Wes rips into his Christmas stocking, which is stuffed with candy and office supplies. Then he dumps the contents of Sofie's stocking onto the floor. From the pile she extracts a package of gummy bears and a tube of Chapstick and withdraws to the sofa. Wes heads for the tree.

I was raised by civilized parents who insisted we take turns opening presents on Christmas morning, but this morning I set that tradition aside. We've spent too much money on too many gifts for the children, so letting the morning spiral out of control into a free-for-all of package ripping feels like the right approach.

Wes tears with violent joy into one box after another.

"Swords!" he cries when he opens the foam swords from Santa.

A few minutes later he's chasing after the dog with a toy chain saw from my mother. I look at the box. Chinese, naturally.

Sofie lolls on the sofa in a stupor from too many gummy bears and applies about 20 coats of Chapstick to her lips. She would have been happy with just those two things under the tree. She has no appetite for opening boxes so I end up opening most of her gifts for her. I get blank looks when I hoist the German dolls and miniature dollhouse accessories at her, but she smiles when I show her what her grandmother sent: a Chinese Hannah Wiggins doll. A frilly pink doll stroller from my sister-in-law, also from China, gets her up off the sofa for the first time in an hour.

I decide it's not so bad to get office supplies for Christmas. The large item from Canada is a chair for my desk, which is not romantic but which I really need because the wooden patio chair I've been using for years is killing my back. The item from Office Depot that had no label about its origins turns out to be a desk calendar. Again, not romantic, but practical, since half the time I don't know what day of the week it is or what I'm supposed to be doing.

Kevin is thrilled with his Cambodian pants.

"These are as good as janitor pants," he beams.

By 9:00 A.M. it's all over. The living room is a riot of wrapping paper and ripped boxes. The morning passes in a fog of excitable holiday phone calls. None of us eats anything but candy.

It isn't until mid-afternoon, with Sofie passed out upstairs, that I have a chance to make a Christmas inventory. Like last year, I pick through the heaps of paper to inspect boxes and tags and compile a list on a notepad as I go. It takes a few minutes, and I have to make a couple of judgment calls, including having to decide whether a coat made in Macau sent to me by my mother counts as Chinese merchandise (I decide that it does), or whether to include items as small as pencil sharpeners and Post-It notes in the final count (I don't).

I sit down to analyze my findings. The count this year comes to China 11, the world 42. Every item with a *Made in China* label comes to us courtesy of my family, including a whopping 60 percent of it from my mother alone. It's not surprising. She never saw the point of the boycott, or maybe she just wanted to make a different point, which is that I can't tell her what to buy for her grandchildren—not that I ever would. Or did.

I get up from the sofa and go to dig around at my desk until I locate last year's Christmas inventory. The count then was China 25, the world 14.

I'm not sure what to make of the numbers. Obviously, our Christmas take is a lot less Chinese than it was a year ago, but it's hard to view the holiday as the culmination of a year of China-free living when Wes is buzzing his Chinese monster truck around the living room and ramming it into the legs of the furniture. It would have been nice to have a tidy end of the year with nothing from China under the tree but, as usual, I'm foiled by the gift exemption. It would have been easier to keep Chinese stuff out of the house if I didn't have relatives, friends, or children, or even the Weakest Link, although he's come around nicely. Then again, maybe I'm just flattering myself, and blaming the family doesn't seem in keeping with the holiday spirit. In any case, you have to work with what you've got.

Across the room, Wes and Kevin sit cross-legged on the floor in a pool of sunshine and dreamily inspect some of the empty gift boxes. They speak in low voices so I have to strain to hear them.

"This one's from Romania," Kevin says, holding up the Tumblin' Monkeys game.

Wes looks thoughtful.

"There sure are a lot of countries I haven't been to," he says.

Kevin holds up the box that held the toy chainsaw that my mother sent.

"This one is from China," he says. "Grandma likes stuff from China, especially chainsaws."

Wes purses his lips, and then says, "I've never been to China but I don't want to go there."

"Why not?"

"Not enough food," Wes answers. "I might get hungry."

He stops to reconsider.

"But they have a lot of toys there, like my monster truck, so maybe we can go there and bring sandwiches."

Wes does not mention that light swords come from China, or the fact that Santa did not bring him one.

■ ■ ■

Two days after Christmas, as we are flying to San Diego to reinvade my parents' house on the pretext of a holiday visit, I notice that something is happening to the Weakest Link. Kevin is gazing out the plane window at west Texas far below us when he turns to me and says, "We should think about sticking with the boycott."

I think, *What?*

I say, *"What?"*

He shifts in his seat and squeezes his eyes meaningfully.

"It's just that it's made us more, you know . . . I don't know," he waves his hands in the air before him. "Thoughtful."

"Thoughtful?"

"In how we spend money," he says.

I turn away from him and study the back of the seat in front of me. This is a surprise. Kevin is getting cold feet about going back to the way things used to be. Jim A., the bitter writer of anti-Chinese letters to the editor, would love this.

I look at Kevin again.

"I thought you couldn't wait to get this thing over with so you could go to Home Depot and buy some Chinese hooks to hang your tools, and then buy some Chinese tools," I say.

He shrugs.

"I had to watch you like a hawk the whole time because I knew you were tempted to sneak around on me," I add. "I thought you hated the boycott."

"I sort of do hate it."

I frown.

"And yet you want to stay with it?"

He shrugs again.

"What about our promise that the kids can choose any three toys they want on New Year's Day, for being good sports?" I ask. "We can't go back on that."

"You mean the Choosing of the Chinese Toys?" he says. "That's a special event that doesn't pertain to what happens next."

He rubs his eyes and then drops his hands to his lap.

"Look, let's not make a decision now," he says. "Just tell me you'll think about it."

■ ■ ■

I do think about it. I think about it off and on for the next four days and I'm still thinking about it at eight o'clock on New Year's Eve as I sit next to Kevin on the sofa in the living room, this time the one in my parents' house.

The reason I'm still thinking about it is that I can't make up my mind about where we should go from here. Kevin's change of heart is a surprise development. I thought that he thought the past year was mostly an exercise in foolishness and a real-time demonstration of just how far he would go to humor me. When I dubbed him the Weakest Link I wasn't kidding, but he turned out to be a better boycotter, and a better sport, than I expected.

I didn't mean to dismiss Kevin's resolve; I just didn't expect him to
have any. I thought keeping clear of Chinese merchandise was all I
could hope for from him. I never expected that the boycott would become meaningful to him along the way. My feeling was that I had run
him down to an emotional nub and there would be nothing left if I
dared to ask for more of no China. I didn't give him enough credit. And
I had missed something about our year that I guess you'd have to call
romance. For me, for love, Kevin bought into my idea and gave up
China for 12 long months.

But is a lifelong China boycott what I really want? I am not at all
certain that it is. On the one hand, it's been satisfying to learn firsthand
that China really hasn't taken over the planet, or our lives, at least not
entirely, although sometimes it looked that way, especially in the toy and
electronics aisles and at the shoe store. Of course, we're not out of the
woods yet. I have a feeling China is just getting started when it comes
to world domination.

On the other hand, we have a broken blender, a stuck kitchen
drawer, and a television that's fading fast, all problems that seem to demand Chinese solutions. We are still boiling water for coffee in the
mornings because we don't have a coffeemaker, and if we don't give up
the boycott then maybe we never will. Lots of little things in life come
from China: birthday candles, squirt guns, light swords. These are small,
inconsequential things that cannot properly be described as important,
but I'm not sure I'd like to live my entire life without them. There's also
the matter of pest control. We smashed our last mouse of the year on
December 26. I'm ready to go back to a catch-and-release approach to
mouse elimination. For that you need a humane mousetrap, and humane mousetraps are made in China.

Besides, the idea of swearing off Chinese products forever feels like
holding a perpetual grudge against 1.3 billion people. I'm not sure I
have the energy for that.

And let's face it: We got through the year mostly by luck. Would I
have had the fortitude to live without a new Chinese television if our
little set had broken early on? Unlikely. And Chinese products made it

in the house on a regular basis despite the boycott, not just through the gift exemption but also through our own bending and breaking of the rules. Kevin cheated on Chinese paintbrushes, among other things, but I've got to own up to a Chinese plastic cooler, mandarin oranges, and Wes's electric pumpkin, not to mention my purchases from Hong Kong and Macau.

Undoubtedly, more bits of China slipped in without our knowing about it, as buttons or plastic bags or components in items whose labels said they were made someplace else. It's possible Kevin snuck in a few things I don't know about, though I doubt it. The guilt would eat him up.

Still, Kevin makes a good point. The boycott made us stop and think before tossing something else in the shopping cart, or at least it did until I got panicky in the weeks before Christmas. It made us thoughtful, and that can't be a bad thing. And there is no doubt the house was cleaner because we stopped filling it up with little things we didn't need but somehow couldn't resist until the boycott made us resist them.

"It's anticlimactic to forget the whole thing," Kevin says as we wait with my parents for the clock to hit midnight in Times Square. "It seems pointless to spend a year doing something and then throw in the towel like the year never happened."

He gives me a disapproving look.

"Do you really just want to go back to our old ways?" he asks. "Won't it make our year a waste of time?"

Yes, I think. Then, no. I have no idea, but one thing is certain. I'm going to have to stop calling Kevin the Weakest Link, if only in my head.

■ ■ ■

Wes wakes bursting with excitement in the wee hours of dawn. All four of us are all crammed into the bedroom I had as a child. It's black as ink outside but Wes knows what's coming with the first light of New Year's Day.

"I'm so happy because tomorrow I'll be able to buy from King Kong," Wes shouts into the darkness.

Kevin shushes him, worried he'll wake my parents.

King Kong?

"What does he know about King Kong?" I whisper to Kevin.

"He means Hong Kong," he whispers back.

My last thought, as I drift to sleep, is to wonder how Wes knew Hong Kong was part of China, when I only recently sorted that out myself.

EPILOGUE

The Choosing of the Chinese Toys takes place on the rainy afternoon of New Year's Day in the children's section of a big bookstore near my parents' house.

We spend a chaotic hour chasing the children through the aisles before heading home with two stuffed animals and a pile of books. Sofie has chosen a white bunny. Wes is clutching a stuffed animal that is either a cat with a dog's body or a dog with a cat's head.

"Dog?" I ask him.

"Cat," he corrects me.

Officially, I am not supposed to know whether the Choosing of the Chinese Toys actually involves Chinese merchandise since I tell the children that our excursion is a special event and I am not going to look at the labels on anything. Unofficially, I can't help myself. That evening, when I'm alone in my old bedroom, I turn over Wes's cat-dog and look at its underside.

Made in China, the tag says.

Just then Wes comes bounding into the room. He's caught me red-handed, with the cat-dog upturned and the label between my fingers.

"You're looking, Mama," he observes.

I decide that he might as well know the truth.

"It's from China," I tell him.

He grabs the cat-dog from my hand and flings it across the room. It lands behind the bed with a thump.

"Shhh," he glares at me. "I don't want him to know."

Sofie's bunny turns out to be Chinese, too, as well as one of her books. After the kids have gone to bed I sit with the Chinese book in my hand and study the words on the flap, *Manufactured in China*. I expect some significant feeling to come over me, either regret or relief, but the only thing that strikes me is how strange it feels to be holding something made in China that we purchased for ourselves.

Kevin looks mournfully over my shoulder at the words on the flap. "A bit of a letdown, don't you think?" he says.

The boycott is officially over. The Choosing of the Chinese Toys is a one-off occasion. We're only hours from January 2 and we haven't yet decided where China fits into the scheme of things in the new year.

■ ■ ■

We are still on vacation in California when a deputy sheriff calls to tell us the Toyota has been recovered, apparently in the same shopping center where it went missing. Doors locked, clean, good condition, he says. Kevin arranges to have it towed to a yard to be checked for damage.

This is good news, but it leaves one question unanswered: Why couldn't Kevin find the car on the night of December 19?

He must know what I'm thinking because when he hangs up the phone he turns and says to me, defensively, "*It wasn't there*. The parking lot wasn't that big to begin with. Somebody must have stolen it and then brought it back."

I tell him that I believe him. I keep to myself the fact that nobody else seems to, including the deputy sheriff who called with the news as well as my mother, who watches us with amusement from across the kitchen.

■ ■ ■

We get another odd call at my parents' house, this time from a Chinese newspaper reporter. The Chinese reporter wants to interview me for a story on our family's year without Chinese goods.

The call from the Chinese reporter is not a complete surprise but it makes me nervous. In late December, the *Christian Science Monitor* ran an essay I wrote about our boycott of Chinese products. Newspapers in Israel, Canada, Dubai, and elsewhere picked up the piece. CBS News sent a film crew to our house the day after Christmas. I was interviewed by National Public Radio.

I wonder if the humor in my piece was lost in translation and whether I'll be labeled an Enemy of the People. I call back the Chinese reporter anyway, more out of curiosity than anything else. He makes quick work of the interview and the next day sends me his story, in Chinese, by e-mail. I send it on to my younger brother for translation.

The reporter has taken some liberties with the spirit of the essay and a few of the facts.

"The children had no toys," my brother translates for me over the phone. "Gone were their laughing, smiling faces."

Not true, I think. Not what I wrote either.

Maybe I should learn my lesson then and there, but I agree to another interview with the Chinese press a week or so later when we have returned from California and I get a call from a Chinese television crew. They spend three hours at our house and Wes falls in love with the camerawoman, who spends an inordinate amount of time filming Wes throwing a ball for the dog as Wes smiles maniacally. Before they leave, they give us a delicate porcelain vase as a gift.

"Check it for a hidden microphone," my worldly neighbor says to me later. "Remember who you are dealing with."

I wave off her concerns. I suppose I should remember that I am playing with fire, even though it doesn't feel like fire at the time. The television crew is charming. The lead reporter is a delicate beauty with a great sense of humor. Her English is perfect. I love her shoes. We hit it off immediately. Our interactions with the Chinese media feel surprisingly normal.

Then I get a call from an aggressive Chinese television reporter who spends the better part of an hour trying to get me to say that the boycott nearly ruined my marriage and my children's happiness and ostracized me from mainstream society. His questions run along these lines:

Wasn't it awkward not buying Chinese items when all your friends were doing it? No.

Did your friends think you were strange? No. They thought we were funny.

Didn't you and your husband fight about this all year long? No, not real fighting.

Didn't this cause a lot of problems in your marriage? No.

Wasn't your husband angry? No.

Weren't your children unhappy because they did not have any toys? No, and they did have some toys, just not Chinese toys.

Didn't you feel sad when you could not buy all the new fashions? No.

Have you ever been to China? No.

What do you know about China? Only what I read in many newspapers and magazines that are available to me through our media.

Then he asks to speak to Kevin.

Didn't you have a lot of fights with your wife because of this? No.

Didn't you feel embarrassed about wearing shoes that did not match? Kevin laughs, then says, emphatically, No.

Weren't you angry with your wife for not letting you buy things from China? No.

And on it goes, rapid-fire, like an interrogation.

After that we have had enough. I stop returning calls and e-mails from the Chinese press. It probably doesn't matter much from their point of view. They have the story they want and they run with it: Americans are so dependent on China for consumer goods that to try to live without them is to pitch your happiness into the wind, is the grim gist of the Chinese media stories. Just look at the difficulties the Bongiorni family faced when they gave it a try. The government media seems to get good play from the story. Months later, when I am on the Internet, I come across a humorless Spanish-language press release titled "Los productos chinos benefician al mundo" ("Chinese products benefit the world") that highlights the world's dependence on Chinese products. Our family story is featured as a cautionary tale.

Maybe I should have listened to my neighbor. Maybe I should have seen this one coming, but in the end it catches me by surprise. I have inadvertently become an instrument of propaganda for the Chinese government. The *red* Chinese government.

■ ■ ■

I get a call about the Toyota from a different deputy sheriff. He's finalizing his crime statistics for December and wants to go over the details of our alleged car theft.

"Now, the car was found in the same place as it was reported stolen, right?" he begins.

"I think so," I tell him.

He goes over the events relating to the car's disappearance.

"So it was stolen from the parking lot where Hooters is?"

Hooters? What's he doing talking about Hooters? No, I tell him, not Hooters. That's four blocks west of the Chinese restaurant. My husband wasn't there, I say. He was at the Chinese restaurant at the opposite end of the boulevard.

"The car was never at that shopping center," I tell the officer.

He's not listening.

"That's not what it says in the report," he counters.

I gently suggest that maybe there is an error in the report if it mentions the center where Hooters is. At that point he drops the Hooters reference and hints at what he really thinks went down on the night in question.

"Don't you think that maybe your husband just had a little too much to drink and couldn't find the car?"

"He had *water*," I say.

I can read his next thought as clearly as if he were speaking the words aloud: *Yes, I imagine that's what he told you, right after he told you he wasn't at Hooters.*

The guy isn't buying my story, which is Kevin's story, which is a true story even if it sounds ridiculous, which I admit that it does. I can understand why the officer is so skeptical. As I listen to my explanations,

I realize I sound lame, like a naïve wife in denial. My voice isn't convincing. I sound uncertain, even to myself. But Kevin is not a let's-get-chicken-wings-at-Hooters sort of a guy, nor is he a lies-to-his-wife sort of a guy. Of course, the deputy sheriff doesn't know that and wouldn't buy it even if I told him that, which I do not.

"But the car was found in good condition?" he asks next.

Yes.

"With the doors locked and nothing missing?"

Correct.

"No trash or damage?"

Right.

I hear him sigh.

"It just doesn't make sense," he says. "That's not how stolen cars turn up."

I agree.

"Look," I say. "My husband says that he came out of the restaurant and walked to where the car was supposed to be and it was gone. He says that unless he is losing his mind that's what happened."

I can tell the guy thinks I'm nuts. Kevin, too.

We go round a few more times until the deputy sheriff has had enough. He tells me he's got to decide one way or another whether a crime took place so he can wrap up his report.

"Don't you think it's possible that maybe your husband just couldn't find the car that night and that it was there all along and somehow he missed it?"

I hesitate. Do I think it's possible? Technically, just about anything is possible.

"*Possible*, yes," I admit. "I just don't think it's *likely*."

He doesn't want to quibble over the difference between possible and likely. He hurries off the phone as soon as he hears me admit that it's possible.

The unsolved mystery of the Toyota is unsettling for two reasons.

First, I still think the Toyota was stolen and that Kevin didn't just misplace it, although by now this is a minority viewpoint, even among our friends and family. The theory that I put forward to my skeptical audience is that some other law-abiding owner of a blue Toyota exactly like ours has a key that fits our car and that they inadvertently drove it a few miles before realizing their error and rapidly reparking it. Probably they were too embarrassed to leave a note. Maybe they had been drinking something besides water that night.

Second, I am not sure what the car's recovery means for the fortune-cookie scandal that I thought I'd unearthed last month. And can the 19th still be considered a lucky day for Kevin?

■ ■ ■

We decide we can live with Chinese imports, sort of.

Swearing off Chinese products forever seems impractical, since it might mean we'd never again buy a cell phone, a squirt gun, or one day maybe even a television. We don't want to give up those things for good.

At the same time, the boycott gave us a discipline that we had lacked as consumers. It was a satisfying experiment. In an unexpected way it made our trips to the mall and the supermarket meaningful, even, at times, fun. Financially, it was probably a wash, since we spent more on some things—Christmas presents, sunglasses—but less on others—shoes and impulse buys, since so often those purchases would have involved Chinese products. We liked spreading our money among a broad field of competitors in the global economy by buying merchandise made in many different countries, including our own.

So we find a middle ground. We decide to look for alternatives to Chinese products when possible but to do business with China when that's the only practical option, which it often is. I put our new guiding principle to work on a small matter in mid-January when I buy the children new toothbrushes, one American and one Chinese. When Kevin orders me a new computer, he discovers the model I want is made in both China and Ireland and requests that they send him an Irish one. They send us one made in China anyway.

In some ways, I am relieved to reunite with Chinese goods. There is Chinese blood in my veins, after all, and in the veins of Wes and Sofie, mixed up with that of nameless Swedes, Italians, Germans, and Irishmen. I don't want to deny my Chinese heritage. It's a proud part of the rootstock of current and future little Bongiornis. Banishing China from our lives forever would feel like closing the door on my Chinese ancestor Mr. Chang, of whom I am very fond. Frankly, his story is the liveliest chapter in the family history so far; I take any opportunity I can to brag about him, to friends and strangers alike. I don't want to give up Mr. Chang, which is what giving up Chinese goods forever might feel like.

■ ■ ■

There is one last bit of unfinished business, a minor matter. It's been just over a year since I replaced the battery in my watch, and I've wondered ever since where the battery was made.

I return to the jewelry store on a quiet morning to replace that battery with a new one. While I wait, I watch an older woman try on enormous diamond rings while her husband looks on with delight. The shopkeeper's wife can't hide her disappointment when I tell her all I need is a new watch battery.

When she reappears with my watch I ask casually if she could tell me where the battery was made. She smiles and ignores my question. I ask it again, twice, in two different ways, until she goes back to check the box.

She's still smiling when she returns and says, "USA."

So that's it. I don't have to add another red mark to my mental list of boycott misdeeds, unless, it dawns on me, this latest watch battery comes from a different box of batteries in the jewelry store's backroom than the one I bought a year ago. Maybe that box was Chinese and only this one is American. I briefly consider trying to sort this out with the shopkeeper's wife, but I'm already back in the Toyota and reversing out of my parking space when I think of it. It will remain a mystery, like the fate of the Toyota itself on the night of December 19. Sorting it out seems like a lost cause.

Of course, you could say the past year was a lost cause, I think as I pull into traffic. But then that defeatist thought gets me nowhere, since the point of the boycott wasn't to beat China, or really to win at anything. It was to try to find our place in the world, and China's place in ours. What I found is that a person can still live without Chinese products, especially if they don't have a rebellious spouse and children or a fixation on cheap shoes and electronics. The fact that we couldn't quite swing it doesn't mean it can't be done at all.

Sometimes I miss the boycott. It feels like we're caving in to something when we buy something with a *Made in China* label. It feels too easy. But trying to live without China sometimes felt the opposite: too hard, at least to stick with for good. And while I am happy to be reunited with my esteemed ancestor Mr. Chang, I confess my feelings about China's place in our lives remain mixed. I like everything to be nice and tidy, but my feelings about China's place in the world, and its place in our home, are complicated.

When I see the words *Made in China*, part of me says, *Good for China*, while another part feels sentimental about something that I've lost, but I'm not sure what exactly. The boycott? The time before the boycott? Maybe something else all together, like lost childhood or the days, about a million years ago, before the term *globalization* was even invented, and when the idea of a China boycott would never have occurred to me in the first place.

I'm afraid I've made things messy for Kevin, too.

"I feel guilty when I buy Chinese things, and then I feel like I'm picking on China when I avoid Chinese things," he tells me.

I may miss the boycott from time to time but I don't know that I'd try it again. In some ways I'd rather not know how much harder life without Chinese goods might be a decade from now. I'm also not sure that I'd want to hear Kevin's answer if I put the question of another China boycott before him somewhere down the road.

After all, you never know. He might say yes.

ABOUT THE AUTHOR

Sara Bongiorni is a writer and former business reporter who has worked at newspapers in California and Louisiana. Her essays and articles have appeared in the *Christian Science Monitor*, the *Shanghai Daily News*, and other publications. *A Year Without "Made in China"* is her first book.

Bongiorni received her undergraduate degree from the University of California, San Diego, and a master's degree in journalism from Indiana University.

She lives in Louisiana, with her husband and three children.

INDEX